# *Lady Balls*

Live Your Ultimate Lifestyle & Build A Business
You Freakin' Love Just By Being *You*

JODY JELAS

*Lady Balls: Live Your Ultimate Lifestyle & Build A Business You Freakin' Love Just By Being You*

© 2015 Jody Jelas

All rights reserved. No part of this publication may be printed, reproduced, stored in a retrieval system, or transmitted, emailed, uploaded in any form or by any means, electronic, mechanical photocopying, recording, or otherwise, without the prior written permission of the publisher.

This publication is sold with the understanding that neither the author or the publisher is engaged in rendering legal, accounting, financial or other professional service. If legal advice or other expert assistance is required, the services of a competent professional person should be sought.

ISBN-13: 978-1511738569
ISBN-10: 1511738561

*Dedicated to the crazy people. The ones who are not afraid to stand out and be themselves. The ones who embrace their dark so that they can shine their light so bright, it magnifies the light in others... for they are the leaders who inspire the world.*

*I love you crazy mofos!*

# A GIFT FOR YOU

To say thank you for reading this book I have put together a gift for you to help you apply the strategies and tools in this book. You can go and grab them right now...

Go grab your free gift at:

**www.ladyballsthebook.com/bonuses**

# CONTENTS

**1 What the F*ck Are LADYBALLS?** ............ 1
**2 What I Want For You (And A Warning)** ............ 5
**3 Why I Wrote This Book** ............ 11
**4 YOU** ............ 19
   Your true identity ............ 20
   Embrace the crazy ............ 23
   Intuition Vs Crazy Voices ............ 24
   Boobs, Heels, & Branding ............ 26
   Heart, Not Head ............ 34
   Happiness is.... ............ 39
   Shit that will stop you ............ 45
   Shit to keep you going ............ 57
**5 Lifestyle by Design** ............ 93
   4 steps to getting what you want ............ 94
   Entrepreneurs Vortex ............ 96
   How To Get More Done ............ 99
   30-Minute Increments ............ 100
   Automate. Delegate. Delete Theory ............ 101

| | |
|---|---|
| Outsourcing | 103 |
| How a House Manager can make you money | 104 |
| 5 Quick Strategies to Generate Cash Fast and Pay For Your House Manager | 107 |
| Parenting & Biz Juggle | 109 |
| Parent Guilt | 112 |
| "Yelly" Parent | 116 |

## 6 Bizniz Time ..................... 119

| | |
|---|---|
| From No List to 5 Figure Days | 120 |
| Your Non-Biz Product Is Valuable | 122 |
| Copying Other People's Shit | 126 |
| Smashing Your Money Blocks | 129 |
| Tsunami of Leads And Momentum | 131 |

## 7 Consistency ..................... 135

| | |
|---|---|
| Consistency | 136 |
| Authenticity | 136 |
| Time | 136 |
| 3-point Check Of A Well-Oiled Sales Funnel | 137 |
| 3 Program Ideas | 139 |
| Business Model Blueprint | 141 |
| Program structure | 144 |
| 3 Low-Hanging Fruit Strategies | 148 |
| Get Ideal Clients Falling Into Your Lap | 150 |
| Tricks To Avoid Toxic Clients | 155 |
| Magnetic Blog—Hot Content Every Time | 159 |

## 8 Uplevel That Shit ..................... 163

# 1

# WHAT THE F*CK ARE LADYBALLS?

# LadyBalls

"**S**trap on a pair!"
"Balls up man!"
"Get some balls!"

All of these phrases are commonly used to define a moment where you have to overcome your fears and step up into your power. Maybe to achieve a goal, or maybe just to do something that scares the shit out of you.

We all know that the most rewarding things yet to be done in life give us two feelings... EXCITEMENT and FEAR!

The things that give you both of those feelings at the same time are the ones you absolutely MUST DO.

I work with both men and women, however, naturally the majority of people I have worked with over the years are women. Most of them are building businesses in a mainly male-dominated industry. I was trying to come up with an acronym for my "BOOM!" program, and the common thread amongst all my clients was that they all had some kind of fear to overcome (we'll be covering some of them in this book).

The B in my BOOM! acronym (in true no-filter-on-this-mouth style) is BALLS. The first thing you need to do to

## What the F*ck Are LADYBALLS?

uplevel your life, grow your business, or pretty much achieve anything, is to strap on your biggest, hairiest set of balls. No matter what you try and do there will always be shit that brings you down. People who don't agree, haters, small-minded people, resistance, or the most terrifying and powerful of all—your own crazy thoughts.

To be able to weather the storm and be the best version of YOU, you need to have BALLS. As I worked with more and more women, it made perfect sense for me to start using "ladyballs" instead of just balls. This is not some man-haters club or anything like that. This book isn't even "Ladies Only". It's just a representation of the first step in smashing through your next glass ceiling to a new level of fl ow and love and creativity.

**So strap on your balls, or your ladyballs—no good ride ever came without the need of a good set!**

# 2

# WHAT I WANT FOR YOU (AND A WARNING)

■ LadyBalls

When I decided to write this book, I had one intention in mind: to be 100% brutally honest and authentic (which includes swearing because that's how I roll). This book reveals some deep, dark, shit about my life, but, most importantly, it also reveals the solutions.

> Someone asked me why I use the 'F' Bomb so much. What the fuck is an 'F' Bomb?

All the juicy things that took me into my brightest light. It's almost more like a series of brain farts that made sense to me at the time. I hope they do for you.

I talk a lot about my journey and my own personal lessons in this book. Not because I want this book to be all about me, but to give you just one perspective. To strap on my "ladyballs" and put myself out there, so that you and whoever you share this book with can learn from it and hopefully enrich your own lives in some way.

What I want for you is to step into your own light and be your 100% authentic self. No filter. No limits. No conforming to others' expectations. Just being your absolute unique self.

## What I Want For You (And A Warning)

# The ballsiest thing you can ever do is to speak your message to the world, openly and loud... for those who need it.

I want you to be so solid in your own self-belief that you will back yourself to the ends of the earth. I want you to have faith in your God-given talents and be invincible to the opinions of others, for they do not define you. Only YOU can define YOU.

You were put on this earth for a reason. Discovering why is a constant journey—learning to embrace the good with the bad, and making the most of it as you go along, so you can have everything you ever desired, and love the process of gett ing there.

I didn't want to write this book as a shiny polished person for good marketing. I see people put others on a pedestal all the time, and then they don't learn from them because they think, "it's all right for you, you are... [insert bullshit here]."

I want to be raw. I want you to see that I'm actually fucking crazy sometimes, and I'm okay with it. We will constantly be learning until the day we die—finding new ways to grow personally, new challenges to process, new opportunities to upgrade our lives and create our "new normal". There is no final destination in life. It's forever changing. It's fluid.

They say there is no such thing as perfect, but there is. It is wherever you are right now. Whatever you are experiencing, good or bad. It's all perfect.

This book is also about creating that lifestyle you have dreamed of your whole life and building a leveraged, scalable business around that desired lifestyle, doing what you truly love. What absolutely blows your skirt up and makes you feel alive every day.

This is not full of quick-win cut-throat strategies to make a shit ton of money fast. This is a lifelong model you can turn into a lifestyle and be proud of. It is designed to be the foundation for the rest of your life.

What I want for you is to finish this book feeling inspired and then take action. Then to pass it on to anyone in your life who you want to inspire into action as well.

This book is from my heart to yours. I genuinely care about you. Really. I do.

## What I Want For You (And A Warning)

No matter what you are wanting in your life (success, love, business, money, spiritual connection) … I know one thing is for sure….

YOU GOT THIS!

> "Always remember: You're braver than you believe, and stronger than you seem, and smarter than you think."
>
> ~AA Milne

# 3
# WHY I WROTE THIS BOOK

# ▎LadyBalls

I *was crying into my keyboard rocking back and forth screaming, "This is not a life!"*

*I was trying to build websites with my right hand.*

*My newborn daughter was in the rocker beside me, and I was rocking her to sleep with my foot.*

*I had the breast milk express pump on my printer trying to get enough milk to feed her for when she woke up, but I was so stressed that my body was not allowing me to provide for my own daughter.*

I would not wish that tornado of emotion on my worst enemy.

I felt useless, incapable, like a bad mother, like a bad business person. I felt like my body was faulty, and I was being punished for something, and that was on top of all the usual stuff that already comes with being a brand new mum.

I was at a loss and didn't know what to do. All of this could have been avoided with one simple realization.

Let me take you back even further....

## Why I Wrote This Book ▌

I started a web design company in 1999 on a plastic desk in my London flat. I was 21 years old, and my goals were basically to make enough money to fly somewhere in Europe and party like a rock star each weekend. I did this many times and had a ball, so I do not regret a single decision I made.

Through my twenties, I had many happy clients, but I had crappy business planning. I had to work my ass off. I nearly went bankrupt twice in my twenties.

It was gut wrenching because I'd studied personal development my whole life. I did my first personal growth program (John Kehoe's *Mind Powers for Teens*) at fourteen years old, and I had enough vision boards to wallpaper the planet three times over.

I cried myself to sleep at twenty-five because I was not a millionaire yet. (If only I knew then that sometimes where there's a will there's a wall and the idea of being in flow).

I was good at what I did and was even one of New Zealand's youngest Businesswoman of the Year finalist for a combination of my business and for the volunteer youth work I was doing in the community.

# LadyBalls

I just made some very poor money decisions that crushed me financially.

The crucial component I was missing... the one thing that would have changed everything... was my WHY.

I didn't have a reason for doing what I was doing. Boozing and partying was not fulfilling in the long run. Clearly, I didn't have enough self-love back then to do it because I deserved success. I made great money but only just enough to have an okay lifestyle—not an exceptional one like I get to have today.

When I had my daughter, everything changed. I had found my why. She was a "surprise" to say the least, but the best surprise anyone could wish for.

I stood back that day from the computer while my daughter slept. I was frustrated enough to finally get my shit sorted.

I asked myself these questions ... (I encourage you to do the same regularly)

- What has worked in the past?
- What has NOT worked in the past?
- What do I LOVE to do in my business?

## Why I Wrote This Book

- What do I HATE to do in my business?
- What truly makes my heart sing?

From that moment forward, I swore that I would not do the things that didn't work. I would do more of that which did work and most importantly… I made a decision to ask myself these questions on a regular basis.

I became the QUEEN of automation and delegation.

I systematized the shit out of my business so tightly (so that I had more free time to enjoy my daughter), other web companies asked me to share my systems with them to replicate, they were so good.

I ended up mentoring (the part I loved) and ditching the web design company (the part I hated).

To this day, I help other people design a LIFESTYLE business that is both leveraged and scalable.

Now, your story will be different, but chances are you are working your ass off and not living the lifestyle you want, otherwise you wouldn't be reading this book.

Through this book, we'll look at your hurdles, your feelings that scream at you for change, and solutions so you

**❚ LadyBalls**

can truly live that epic lifestyle that you've dreamed of since you were a little kid.

> Something very beautiful happens to people when their world has fallen apart: a humility, a nobility, a higher intelligence emerges.

There are 4 crucial components to living the lifestyle you want and having a business that you love. We will cover them all in this book.

- ❚ YOU — Being 100% yourself and defining your true identity.
- ❚ LIFESTYLE — Design your ultimate lifestyle and overcome any barriers or beliefs that stop you having it.
- ❚ BUSINESS — Execute the business model that supports your new lifestyle so you can be free and love what you do again.
- ❚ UPLEVEL — Once it's all in place, see what else you can do to constantly uplevel and give back to others.

## Why I Wrote This Book

That lifestyle you deserve; the one that the Universe is waiting for you to commit to so it can roll out the red carpet and have it come to you with ease and grace. It's just waiting on you!

# 4

**YOU**

■ LadyBalls

> The greatest freedom in the world is to be who you truly are. No filters. No limits.

## Your true identity

So often we lose ourselves in our roles as mother, father, partner, daughter, son, sibling, boss, community member. We forget what we truly want and try to fit a square peg into a round hole, trying to please everyone else except ourselves.

They say that for people on their deathbeds, the most common response when asked their biggest regrets, is that they wish they'd done more for themselves.

Getting super clear on who you are, your true identity, is crucial to living a fulfilled and happy life.

Not trying to fit into the expectations, beliefs, or stereotypes of people around us, or any external forces.

When you are aligned with your true identity, you jump out of bed each day with a skip in your step.

You are full of joy, and you feel alive! You are creative and have the power to be, do, and have anything you

## YOU

want for your life. Your vibe is infectious and therefore rubs off on others around you, which in turn increases their happiness purely through inspiration.

It doesn't matter what your life circumstances are, even in the down times. If you are 100% true to the person you want to be, then even when times are tough (and let's face it—shit happens), you will be proud of who you are and enjoy contentment and peace like no other.

You will be able to create any new normal you wish to create for yourself.

When you are 100% yourself, totally raw, with no filter, you are truly living with authenticity.

Not only does this make you feel good for being true to yourself, but in turn it allows others to trust you, as well.

There is an added bonus to being 100% yourself when it comes to business. People buy from people they trust. You can't fake authenticity. People can smell falsity a mile away.

Authenticity includes being true to yourself, as well. Being true to your values, what's important to you, and to stand in your power.

# LadyBalls

It's too easy to get sucked into the "tall poppy syndrome" and play a small game in life. Beginning when we are young, we are told, *"stop trying to be the center of attention"* and *"be humble"*. Too many people are too scared to shine, so they are depriving the world of their wisdom and teachings.

You have more raw talent hidden than you can even imagine. Everyone does. We only ever tap into a small portion of that. The truth is that every one of us has a brilliance that the world needs. You just have to find what YOUR gifts are and step up to the plate.

Even if your value is helping others, at the end of the day you must take care of #1 first. YOU. You are no use to anyone if you don't put yourself first. I've done it myself working for charities and nearly losing my business. I've seen people focusing so much on others that their own family and health suffers. Self-love comes first. Period.

## Being selfless is a nice idea, but if focusing only on others makes you burnt out, sick, and broke, then you are not being the leader you need to be to truly help others.

## Embrace the crazy

> "When there is no enemy within, the enemies outside cannot hurt you."
>
> ~ **African Proverb**

Let's face it. Sometimes, when you're alone with your thoughts, you come up with some weird shit. You think that if someone were to hear that on the outside, they may have you locked up in an insane asylum.

With some of the shit I come up with, I find myself in fits of laughter thinking, *"where the hell did that come from?"* It's both a blessing and a curse. A blessing because it means I'm in a creative flow, but a curse because I can make up shit and have it seem so real that I have to have a good chat with myself to work out what's truth and what's crazy.

The truth is, we all have a little crazy in us—a dark side, negative thoughts, that devil on your shoulder, a destructive little voice in our heads. It's "normal".

It's when we pretend the crazy doesn't exist, or ignore it, or judge ourselves for it, that it becomes evil.

# LadyBalls

> I have finally mastered how to tell which voice is just my crazy neurotic head talk and which is actually my trusty intuition.

Without the dark, there are no stars. We wouldn't know light without the dark. If all we had were good days, how would we know that they were good days without the bad ones to compare them to?

We'd never learn a thing if everything was just rainbows and butterflies. There is no fun in that!

After all, they say the crazy ones are the ones who change the world, right?

## Intuition Vs Crazy Voices

Every time I get in a spin, I just have to trust the process. Instead of listening to the crazy neurotic voice, I listen another layer deeper, and there I hear my trusty intuition. The crazy voice is one of fear, insecurity, jealousy, lack of trust, scarcity, and it doesn't serve me. It releases some weird invisible-feeling juices into my body that send me on a depressing downward spiral of bullshit.

## YOU ∎

The only way to keep your head above water in this kind of instance is to first embrace that we all have a little crazy. It's part of who we are, so love it. Don't feel guilty or insane for having a little bit of *"Me, Myself & Irene"* in you.

The second part is to dull the crazy voices for a second by going within, one layer deeper.

Now listen again. Listen to the sweet voice of intuition. The one telling you the other voice is just your fears from the past. It's just stories you have made up from your past experiences that you then turned into a belief. It's not real.

Past that voice is the voice of truth. It's a voice of love, support and encouragement. There is clarity there, and it's factual and simple.

**When you learn to quiet your mind of the crazy voices... you can hear.**

**DOWNLOAD THE IDENTITY EXERCISE for free at:
www.ladyballsthebook.com/bonuses**

■ LadyBalls

## Boobs, Heels, & Branding

There was a major turning point in my life when I stood up and into my own authenticity. It was a life-changing moment, and I'm very passionate about it. I feel a fire in belly just thinking about it, and I LOVE IT!

But first, I need to clarify MY definition of BRANDING. Branding to me is not just your logo or the design of your website.... it's more than that.... It's how everything about YOU and your business is portrayed to the world.

BUT I have a little problem with that. Sure, I think it's important that your market thinks you are professional, but one person's perception of what professional is may be very different from the next man's.

I've always had issues with my over-all brand. I'm a female in an industry of mostly men. Being a blonde big-boobed female has a bunch of stereotypical beliefs attached to it.

A few years back when I was moving more into coaching and developing my Jody Jelas brand, I asked for feedback on people's perception of me based on my photo and logo (no video or content—just a photo).

# YOU

The response was: *"People will not take you seriously because you're all boobs and heels"*. No joke.

That was a pivotal moment for me in my business and here's why.

Firstly.... I had just spent a few days defining WHY I was moving into coaching and what my business meant to me. Because at the end of the day, I wanted this to be a lifestyle choice. I wanted to do what I love and enjoy it. I wanted the freedom to be myself and not worry about what others think. If I was proud of what I did and made a difference, then THAT is what truly mattered to me.

> "Care about what other people think, and you will always be their prisoner."
>
> **~Lao Tzu**

I was over working for other people or having people dictate what I can and can't say or do.

My entire life, my appearance, especially my boobs, has caused so many issues.

# LadyBalls

As a little four-year-old girl, I remember strutting proudly up my street in my new yellow dress like I was on a stage. Everything to me was a stage. The trampoline. A pile of wood. I just saw myself standing up and entertaining or leading. But I was always being told not to be the center of attention, so I started to feel like being myself was a bad thing, and I should be more like what people wanted of me.

I was bullied by girls from when I was eleven because I had to wear a bra when no one else did yet. Girls I didn't know used to call my Nana's phone and shout into the phone that they were going to kill me. At Saturday sports, I'd get hit in the head in the tuck shop line for no reason. I was good at sports, so I had lots of male friends, but after puberty that switched to them wanting more. I remember four boys holding me down and ripping my clothes off, throwing them on top of the tennis club.

Even when it came to breastfeeding my kids, I had problems with my boobs. They didn't seem to be helping me out as they should have then, either.

So the day that the coach said that people will only ever see boobs and heels, I made a decision. To this day, it is one that had the biggest impact. I will no longer allow my life to be dictated by other people's bullshit.

## YOU ∎

My business is to serve people. People who I can TRULY help and care for. I want to make a difference in people's lives by helping them feel free to be themselves and to take their business to new heights that they would not otherwise have experienced.

I want them to experience freedom, (whatever that is for them) just as I do. That's the legacy I want to leave.

> **Contentment: When your own life (not something or someone external) brings a smile to your face every day.**

I ONLY want to work with the people I love to serve, and I will do everything in my power to inspire and lead them to live the life they truly want for themselves.

When you're in business for yourself, when it comes to your clients (and this goes for ANY relationships you're in, both biz and personal), you should always respect them.

BUT there is ONE person you should always respect and love above all else, no matter what..... and that is YOU.

# LadyBalls

It is YOUR brand. YOUR business. YOUR life. If you like to have your life dictated by other people and their opinions and allow their bullshit to rule your life, then DON'T BECOME AN ENTREPRENEUR.

Haters gonna hate, baby! And people are always going to want to check in their ninety cents.

Design a business that is everything YOU want. Define the type of cool people YOU want to work with. Do the work to attract those people into your life, and serve them!

I decided from that day on, I would never let anyone make me feel bad about who I was and how I looked. I would stand tall, shoulders back, and if they like me and I can help them, then I'll bend over backwards to do it. If they are negative and don't like who I am, then I don't need them in my life.

Surround yourself with people that make you the best version of yourself.

There are days when someone might throw me off my game for a bit, but only for a second, and I keep coming back to that crucial center point. Only I can be responsible for how I feel in each moment. We can never

## YOU

control the external, only what we feel within ourselves and how we respond.

When it comes to branding this may all sound like a contradiction, seeing as I love me some good graphic design, and I like things pretty—I'm not saying don't put in any effort to have your stuff look great. If that's important to you, then do it! I do!

What I am saying is.... focus on putting out great stuff that helps people.

Don't waste weeks trying to decide what is the right shade of blue for your site. You're in business to make money. Ask yourself this question every day: "Is what I'm doing right now moving me towards my ultimate lifestyle?"

Anyone who won't work with you because your blue is a little too teal for their liking.... NOT AN IDEAL CLIENT.

Anyone who judges you for using words like GUNA or for misspelling.... NOT IDEAL.

If people watch an inspiring ten minute video right to the end and then pull you up on a tiny little mistake in it instead of focusing on the message.... NOT IDEAL.

# LadyBalls

I'm a self-confessed terrible speller. I have my own world of slang that I get pulled up on all the time. But if you meet me.... that's how I talk. No filter. Just transparent and straight up.

SURE, I don't always speak good ENGLAND (see what I did there) AND yes I'm blonde and have big boobs!

(I know—women have BOOBS! can you believe it?) Don't trust anything with boobs! ;) .... but this is me. Genuine.

I had a client tell me that someone asked him to speak at a meeting, but that he should change his brand to make it LOOK like there is more than just HIM in his business.

My advice...... Don't change your business to suit another person or company. It's YOUR BIZ and your terms.

## Never be afraid to be yourself. If you try to be something else, you're a fake!

Lifestyle business is about the freedom to be yourself.

## YOU ∎

If your content is good, your message and goals clear, then that is what's really important. A one hundred dollar bill screwed up and dirty is still worth one hundred bucks.

So when you're defining who you want your brand to be about....... BE YOURSELF. Then you'll ALWAYS be unique :) Competition will not even be a thought. There is only one you.

Whatever you have heard your whole life that has held you back—those are OTHER people's beliefs! These may have come from your childhood that you now hear yourself saying all the time.

> **Beliefs are just your perceptions based on experiences. You can seed a new belief and solidify it by creating new.**

So what do you choose as your new normal?

**▌ LadyBalls**

## Heart, Not Head

Guts spilling begins.... I've always been so tough. At least, that is how I tried to come across. It's a protection mechanism.

I developed beliefs when I was very young to not let anyone have any power over me. I made a decision that I needed no one. I was better off on my own. I could look after myself. I didn't need any help because I could only trust myself. I had control of me.

I decided I would never allow myself to become vulnerable. I saw it as a weakness.

Studying personal development my whole life has been important, but in a way, I also used it as a way to keep people out. I mastered my mind so well that my physical pain threshold is ridiculously high, and 99% of the time, I can trick my mind into all sorts of things. No other person can infiltrate my mind. I am its master.

It's all BULLSHIT.

# YOU ∎

## Mastering the mind is easy compared to letting down your walls and mastering the heart... but that's a whole other fucking Oprah show!

I'm not just talking about relationships with others, but in all areas. My business, communication with people and most of all, love for myself.

I had deprived myself for so many years of so much love. Building my walls up so high, I never got to truly enjoy life through full self-expression. It was like being trapped frozen for thirty years, but still being able to think and feel, being fully conscious.

I remember at high school people calling me *"the girl who you don't hug"*. I would run from hugs... when really all I wanted was someone to hug me and say, *"It's okay. It's not your fault. You got this."*

Really, underneath my "strong" exterior, I'm a big softy. Always have been. I care for people so genuinely that my heart can be overflowing with love and broken all in one day. I'm a fucking roller coaster of intense emotion, and I'm okay with it. The people who are im-

# LadyBalls

portant in my life, and the people who I can serve by being my hardcore authentic self, will embrace it as I do.

They will be inspired to embrace their own dark and light. I hope by "LadyBallsing up" and putting this out there (wearing my heart on my sleeve), others will have the courage to do the same.

I cry when I'm proud, I cry when overjoyed, I cry in kids' movies, I cry when I'm inspired, I cry if someone holds a hug for a little over the "acceptable" time, I cry when a client has a breakthrough... Hell, I've cried at the pure beauty of a sunset. Like I'd just been handed an invaluable gift that I'm so grateful for, and I'm watch-ing it unwrap itself.

When I'm upset or mad and can't smash the shit out of a kickbag or pads, my outlet is to cry. That shit's gotta get out somehow! Sometimes I wrestle with my demons. Other times we just snuggle.

In 2014, I had some challenging times, and it really tested who I was being. I made a very clear distinction on who I wanted to be, no matter what came at me. After all, I have a fucking great life. There was just one thing I needed to master... and that was the affairs of the heart.

## YOU

After a coaching session with one of my mentors, Marci Lock, I made a commitment to myself to live from that day with my walls down. To wake up each day and make a conscious decision to come from a place of love. And while on a Bali trip, in a conversation with my bestie Victoria Gibson, it finally became clear to me.

In my business and in relationships, I always lived with one leg in the door with a solid strong foundation, but the other leg was always out the door ready to run for the hills at the slightest chance of things not working. Like a gammy leg of fear. Haha!

There was stuff I was meant to be teaching to clients who I were mentoring that I was too scared to commit to myself. I stuck to sales funnels and video marketing as a safe place. It was all metrics, and I could control it. I was depriving them of the other crucial learning stuff I was more than equipped to help them with that were far more life-changing than just making money.

> When your fears hold you back from sharing your genius, you are depriving all the people who really need you.

# LadyBalls

I was the same in my relationships. I would run from or sabotage any opportunity so that I would end up alone again... my safe place... my comfort zone.

The new "walls down" me came purely from a place of love. Even if I was let down, hurt, or failed, handling a hater, anything in any area of my life, I would STILL come from a place of love. I would have an understanding that as long as I made decisions that made me proud of myself, I could never go wrong.

After decades of being the "tough" one, I had let the steel, thick walls surrounding my heart down, and I was exercising it.

It has been like doing Crossfit for the first time and going hard on a new muscle you don't think you have ever used before. It's fucking uncomfortable, but if you just keep working at it, it will become big and strong. I've since done a "harmony integration" session with Satyen Raja and solidified that flow and creativity at an even deeper level.

Since making that decision, my entire business has changed. I feel like I am seriously fulfilling my purpose. I am so overjoyed at the breakthroughs I see clients have that I feel like I am FINALLY making a difference and leaving my legacy to the world.

## YOU ∎

I know now that coming from a place of vulnerability is not a weakness at all. In fact, it is actually a strength. In fact, vulnerability is the greatest strength of all.

**When we allow ourselves to be 100% authentic and express ourselves from a place of love...**

**...only then do we truly experience peace and joy.**

I wish that for everyone.

---

**TAKE THE FEAR TEST**
**and discover what you need to release to move forward with confidence.**
**It's free over at:**
**www.ladyballsthebook.com/bonuses**

## Happiness is....

We all seek happiness. We search for that state of being. We hope that one day we will reach it as if it's a final destination, and once we reach that place, our lives will be perfect forever. We will be 100% happy all the time. Like a fairytale that we don't honestly believe will ever come true.

That's because it's bullshit. You need the shit as well.

We try so hard to be happy.

We try so hard to NOT be UNhappy.

We try to create situations that give us that good feeling temporarily, like getting drunk or taking drugs to make us happy. All that does is mask the things that keep us UNhappy and stops us from discovering what keeps us in a state of misery.

I love to have a few drinks, don't get me wrong. Having a few drinks is fine, but not to mask misery. In fact, drinking only magnifies my current emotion, so if I was miserable and went off to drink, it would only make me more miserable.

## YOU

If we numb the messages our minds and bodies give us, how will we ever enjoy true moments of happiness? They'll just be false feelings. We will be jumping from pretend joy state to pretend joy state, until next thing we know, we are dead and gone and have never truly lived.

We try so hard to find happiness that it's like chasing rainbows. The harder we try, the more elusive happiness is.

When we are truly happy…. it's like some freaky happiness juice is released into our brain. In that moment nothing else in the world matters. Nothing can break our joy.

Think of those times as a kid when you were so in the moment that everything in your world seems perfect. Pure, untarnished joy.

> "Sometimes your joy is the source of your smile, but sometimes your smile can be the source of your joy."
> ~THICH NHaT HaNH

# LadyBalls

I can think of a time when I was four, riding my bike around the neighborhood (with just my bikini bottom on because I wanted to be one of the boys), singing to myself, and being so in the moment that time flew by.

I recall a time, when I was about fifteen, I was boogie boarding at the beach alone, again singing to myself, and before I knew it, it was dark, and my mum had sent someone down to get me to come home. I'd been there for so long that half a day went by. I think that was one of the happiest moments of my life. I had a very colorful teenage journey, so that moment truly stands out to me. I found something that I loved so much, and was so passionate about in that moment, that all my troubles vanished.

In my adult life, my happy place is snorkeling. I associate the ocean with limitlessness. If I ever find myself playing small or not being able to see a solution to a challenge, I will go to the ocean and look out. When I look at the horizon, to me that is infinity. It puts things in perspective for me. Its grandness is so much bigger than any problem I could face.

So when I'm snorkeling and exploring the wonders of the sea, I'll sing to myself underwater. I remember being on a girl's trip in Egypt, snorkeling at the Blue Hole near Dahab, and I was so into the moment that I found myself surrounded by jellyfish.

## YOU ■

I was about twenty meters from the group and so into experiencing the joy of the moment that I had no recollection of how I got so far away from everyone. Then I was afraid the jellyfish would get me, so I dived down as deep as I could and kicked my fins like a mermaid on steroids to get the fuck out of dodge, haha!

For the parents... those moments when you are staring into your new baby's eyes thinking.... how you never thought you could love something so fucking much. At the same time thinking... I have no idea what the hell I'm doing! :)

For the party people.... When I'm dancing like a crazy person on a dance floor with a grin from ear to ear letting loose.... I lose myself in the moment and nothing else matters. And then when the DJ drops one of my favourite tunes.... Oh my God. Shit gets cray. My friends know me for two phrases. First, "*Hey I've got that font*" and secondly, "*Oh my God—this is my jam!*" Which is usually followed by helicopter dancing that clears a dance floor faster than a suspicious bag at an airport.

Seriously... I'm surprised no one has lost an eye! What about those moments when you laugh so hard it hurts?

■ LadyBalls

## If love is the treasure, laughter is the key.

As we become adults, we seem to let our fears and beliefs and the expectations of others block those feelings of joy.

A person who truly experiences that child-like joy understands that happiness is not a destination. Happiness is about being present in every moment. It is the ability to not worry about the future or dwell on the past. It's about right now. When they are learning, inspiring, playing, dancing, laughing, they are happy but they also know that the moments of fear, misery, confusion, and feeling lost is ALL part of it as well!

If we were happy all the time, we wouldn't even know what happiness was. We'd be immune to it.

The happiest people in the world are often the people who have been through the most crap! Sometimes the suffering is where true joy comes from.

Now is a moment. In a few seconds… that is a moment. It is learning to embrace ALL those moments (good and bad) that create the contrast so we know what happiness is. It's about dropping everything, letting go, and

## YOU ∎

truly feeling the experience in the moment with no fear and no judgement.

Happiness is not a place we get to and then it's all over. Happiness is in the small moments. It's appreciating all the little things that make our hearts giggle. It's the thing that makes us forget everything for a second and be 100% there. 100% present. Having this awareness means you can CHOOSE your state in any situation.

What are those childhood memories of pure happiness for you? When was the last time you did that as an adult?

Write down all the happiest moments of your entire life and when the shit hits the fan go back and read them. I bet you'll grin like a kid at Christmas, and in that state of remembering joy, it's impossible to experience misery.

Do more things that make you laugh so much that your sides hurt and you think you will throw up.

Joy is infectious, too. As you experience more joy in your life, those around you will automatically reap the rewards of your happiness, too. It's science ;) Surround yourself with people who make you feel joyful.

You owe it to yourself to choose happiness.

■ LadyBalls

> "Looks like everybody's kicked a goal."
> ~**Daryl Kerrigan,**
> the movie, "The Castle"

## Shit that will stop you

### YOUR FEARS: A Snake or a Rope?

Byron Katie tells a story of being on a hike in the desert and coming across a rattlesnake. Her heart felt like it had stopped, and she could not even bring herself to look back at the snake. She imagined that they would find her body in the middle of the secluded desert with no one to hear her screams for help.

She then somehow mustered up the courage to glance back at the snake, and realized that the snake was actually a rope. She fell to her knees, laughing and crying with relief.

She knew she was safe. She knew she could stand over the rope for one thousand years and never fear it again. The entire world could come across the snake and scream and scare themselves to death, but she would never again fear that snake.

There is nothing that could make her fear that "snake" ever again.

This is with all our fears.

**Fears are not real. They are an illusion. A perception.**

Fear is something that is made up in our heads (based on the past), and once we realize this, we can free ourselves from the fear and live a joyous life, never to fear that thing again.

What is it that is scaring the hell out of you in your life? What makes your stomach turn and has your heart in knots?

The truth is that it's just a FEELING you have created inside your mind, which sends the message to your body. Probably just based on something that has happened in your life or something you witnessed.

Your past is not your future. If you had amnesia and started again, you wouldn't fear half the stuff you do now.

What if that fear was not at all the truth?

What if that "snake" was just a "rope"?

At the end of the day the truth is: "The snake IS a rope."

# LadyBalls

### Why Playing Below 100% Is The Loneliest Place In The World

Life can sometimes be so easy. Everything just falls into place. On the other hand, sometimes life can throw you a shit sandwich. A whirlwind of challenges, or as I prefer to call it, GROWTH OPPORTUNITIES.

This can only mean one thing... the calm before the Tsunami of Awesomesauce: where everything is in flow and good things just flow to you with ease!

> Sometimes before the Up-Levelling. Comes a storm. Trust the process.

Making these massive shifts in my own life came with a few days of shit turning upside down! I didn't sleep, my throat hurt, I kept ramming bad food in my gob, and then I realized that it was just resistance kicking my ass because I was breaking through the highest glass ceiling I had ever broken through! An emotional barrier I'd lived with had limited me my entire life. Bullshit I'd carried right from being a little girl.

Now we all have our bullshit, but for me... and I'm being brutally honest here... I grew up with the belief that playing at 100% meant being alone. Being isolated

## YOU

from others because they would get jealous, intimidated, or just straight up feel small because I was playing big. Believing that it truly is "lonely at the top" (which is bullshit of course).

So to avoid being alone my whole life, I always played at 60%. That 60% did me well, but imagine what a difference we could all make in the world if we would just go all in and play at 100%. We were born with abilities and gifts that can change lives and literally change the world. Who the hell are we to play so small?

In my recent growth, I've realized that on the other side of 60% is a group of other amazing people on the same high level, all-in journey. People who lift each other up, not drag each other down. I also realized I had it the wrong way around. Playing at 60% was the loneliest place. I was not playing full out.

The other thing I've done my whole life is hold the false belief that FIERCE INDEPENDENCE would get me through life. Trust no one. Do everything on my own. I can conquer the world just with me. But that, too, is bullshit!

[SIDE NOTE: If anyone needs any help in moving house on your own I've stubbornly done it many times and could write a book of tricks. Like moving a fridge

# LadyBalls

on a piece of cardboard, using your heels as a hammer and a nail file, which doubles as a flathead AND phillips screw driver.]

It's all good to be independent but not to the detriment of your business, your life, or (for me) relationships.

> No one wants to be in a relationship where they feel like an outsider because you are too busy saying, "Fuck you, World— I have this on my own and I don't need you."

So I want to ask you a question: in all the areas of your life... how IN are you?

Even if you are already a high achiever, I bet there is STILL room for more! Still room for the most absolute epic life that you can imagine, and the only thing between YOU and YOUR DREAM LIFE is the bullshit.

Now you know I love me some ballsy straight up naked authenticity. So I dare you to get RAW! I dare you to write down what YOUR limiting belief is that has held you back. By ballsying up and putting it out there on paper, you are making a commitment to yourself to address it and prove those old beliefs wrong.

Then, create a new belief that is empowering, and take actions every day that make that new empowering belief your new truth!

### Fear Of Putting Yourself Out There

WOW! Amazing what comes up when you put yourself out there!

> What if they don't like me? What if I'm not good at what I do? So many people are already doing this!

Straight up—some people won't like you. That's none of your business, though.

Truth is, you might not be the best at what you do, but I guarantee you know more than some people, and they are the ones you can help.

99% of the time there IS someone doing it. But they are not you and never will be. You will have your own personality and spin that you put on it that makes what you share so unique.

### ▍LadyBalls

Some time ago, I did a product launch with ads and lots of activity on Facebook. It brought about a woman trying to bring up personal stuff from my past near-bankruptcy (which I address in my videos all the time because I'm committed to transparency), but on the other hand...

I have also had the most wonderful emails from people who have watched my videos and been inspired and got great results! I've had some real tear-jerker messages from people saying I've changed their lives. (but really it was all them—I was just a guide).

A lot of people fear putting themselves out there because of what it may bring up for them, either from others, or just their own internal self-limiting beliefs.

To get your message and wisdom out to the world, you gotta be able to put yourself out there. If you're 100% transparent in your story and your message, and what you are offering the world will bring GOOD to their lives, then it is your duty to do it!

DON'T HIDE!

I GUARANTEE THERE WILL BE HATERS! I GUARANTEE THERE WILL BE CREEPY PEOPLE!

But I also GUARANTEE that if you are WORKING TO ASSIST OTHERS, then everything will work out exactly how it's meant to!

Focus on you and being your best. Then everything else will just fall into place perfectly and in perfect time.

KEEP DOING YOUR BIT TO MAKE THE WORLD BETTER, PEOPLE HAPPIER, and MORE EPICALLY ABUNDANT!

When people are hating and try to pull you down, it is not because YOU are bad. It is because you playing BIG scares the shit out of them and heightens THEIR INSECURITIES. Their own BULLSHIT!

THAT IS NOT YOUR ISSUE!

In fact, after an amazing discussion with that person who was trying to bring me down on Facebook, the conversation ended with her saying it was her own self-limiting beliefs (TRUST NO ONE) that had her doing that. She also clarified that she'd followed me for a long time and has seen me mention my past challenges.

■ LadyBalls

STAND STRONG IN YOUR MESSAGE. BELIEVE IN YOURSELF AND WHAT YOU DELIVER.

Continue to do your part to bring happiness, wealth, inspiration and general good vibes to this world.

> Kindness: Sprinkle that shit everywhere! Amen.

### Paradigms

WHAT WILL YOU SETTLE FOR?

My Dad and I were once the only Certified Leaders in New Zealand to teach Bob Proctor, Michael Beckwith and Jack Canfield's *Science of Getting Rich* teachings. We held weekly events in Auckland City sharing what we'd been trained to teach.

Bob Proctor talks a lot about "Paradigm shifts". These are deep root beliefs that influence us every day.

This explanation was perfect: Paradigms are like gates. Some are easy to open and get through. Others have been there so goddamn long that they are rusted up and so fucking "hard" to shift. It's like you're so stuck in

**YOU** ∎

that limiting belief it "feels" like it's become part of who you are.

IT'S NOT! A gate is a gate and can be opened. It may take a wrench or a grunty chainsaw to break through that MOFO but at the end of the day...

IT CAN BE SHIFTED.

New beliefs can be seeded and grow. Beliefs that SERVE you rather than keep you STUCK in mediocrity.

There is no reason to settle for good when you can have GREAT!

> There is no reason to settle for **MEDIOCRITY** when you can have **EPICNESS!**

Okay, okay. You can settle, but settle for this.....

A LIFE THAT IS NOTHING SHORT OF FUCKING EX-TRAORDINARY!

### Don't Do It Alone

Some of us can be so stubbornly independent that we think that we don't need anyone else.

The most important thing I ever did to turn my business around was to commit to a mentor. This not only gives you the best support in whatever it is you need support with, but it also means that you are backing yourself.

> "The soil says 'Don't bring me your need—Bring me your seed'."
> ~ Jim Rohn

If you are willing to invest a good chunk of money in a mentor, then it's because you believe in yourself enough to make a change.

My mentor Kevin Nations was the best investment I ever made. He believed in me even when I didn't believe in myself. His wisdom and support helped me in every area of my life, and I will forever be grateful for the change he ignited in me.

One thing he did teach me is how to make the most of mentoring, as well. A good mentor will not listen to you bitch and moan with excuses. They are there to help you find a solution, so you can move forward and be your best.

Invest in a mentor who you resonate with. If the amount of money you are investing scares the crap out of you, then even better!

I will never be without mentors. Every great achiever has had some form of coach or mentor.

## Shit to keep you going

### *Persistence—New Normals You Are Blind To See*

When I asked my good friend, Nat Tolhopf, what she thought would be powerful to add to this book, she said I should write about persistence. I had to ask her what the hell I would write about persistence. Here is what she said:

*"You never give up. Your calling is strong. You don't lis-ten to the naysayers, you surround yourself with people who believe in you, and you say fuck you to the world."*

When she said that to me my reaction was, *"Of course — goes without saying".*

# LadyBalls

It was then that I realized that never quitting on something I feel strongly about is just in my DNA now. It's second nature.

It was not always that way.

Most of my life, I would put the pedal to the metal and go hard and fast on whatever I was working on, then when things got tough, I'd pull back and end up with a half-pie attempt. It was kinda like that meme, "It's fuck-this-shit o'clock!"

But when I had the breakthrough with the whole "Boobs & Heels" story, when I finally got clear on my values and who I wanted to show up as in my life, I never looked back.

I knew the road would be bumpy, and it might change course, but as long as I stayed true to what was important to me, there was no quitting. I just wanted to inspire others, be 100% myself and be a person of action. Whatever I do in my life, as long as I stay true to that, then I was leaving a legacy and I would be proud of who I was.

# YOU

**Normal is fluid. It's whatever reality you choose it to be and you can shift your normal at any moment. Set your sights on a life you love and step into YOUR new normal.**

It was beautiful to see how something that used to be far from a good habit of mine become engrained in me and is now who I am... the person who is persistent and never gives up.... that it was my new normal.

We all have habits we wish we had in our lives. The truth is, we CAN learn those habits. As with the muscle you work at the gym—you do anything enough times and it eventually become standard.

The perfect example of this is how I've been learning to surf, recently. The first trainer showed me the technique he knew to stand up on the board. *"Three steps and pop up fast"* he said. *"Then bend your knees and look at the shore."*

The next trainer I had showed me a totally different way to "pop up" on the board. I found that one easier and mastered that part, but I hadn't mastered staying up on the board.

# LadyBalls

He, too, said to bend your knees and eyes to the shore. Once I eventually sussed the getting up part, it became second nature. I could get up easily enough, but next I had to suss out the bended knees. Once I started to nail that, I could focus on the eyes on the shore.

Practice. Practice. Practice until it all becomes natural. This goes with ANYTHING. Learning new skills, mas-tering our minds, developing new habits. If we could magically install a program into our heads like in the *Matrix* movie, we'd be sorted but that's not how it works (yet). So instead, we have to train ourselves.

You can only fail if you quit!
CONSISTENT PERSISTENCE.
Keep going until you win!

### Seat Belt Theory

Trapped. Blind. Stuck. Frustrated!?

Where the FUCK are all the solutions???

Let it go. Let it flow.

## YOU ∎

I'm about to tell you what the hell seat belts have to do with making moves in your business, and the ONE THING that you can do to free yourself from the crap and really uplevel ya shizzle!

I'm guna tell you a true story. An incident that is the perfect metaphor for what we are like when we are stuck!

I was running late with my kids to go to the movies one day. They were both excited, but if we didn't hurry the hell up we were guna miss the start! The kids jumped into the car—we were all frazzled. My kids have this fear (a good fear) where they start freakin out about the car even being ON when they don't have their seat belts on.

My six-year-old Milly is panicking. I'm slowly backing out of the driveway putt ing a bit of pressure on her, and her seat belt won't budge. She starts screaming and going crazy. She was completely blind to the solution because she was in such a crazy state of panic.

Now I could see from the front seat that the seatbelt was twisted, she was pulling it to hard and fast. If she let it go and pulled it slowly and untwisted it—BOOM! Solution!

I just kept saying to her, *"take a breath. I'm not going anywhere. You need to find a solution and that will only happen if you are calm and breathing."*

## LadyBalls

I didn't want to GIVE her the solution. I saw it as the perfect way to teach her about what your state of mind can do to you, and how if you learn to manage those crazy moments, then solutions WILL flow to you.

She STILL didn't calm down. So I said, *"how much do you want to see this movie?"* —obviously the reply was *"real bad!"*

I continued, *"so if you want to see this movie so bad, you need to take a breath, and find a solution or else we don't leave this driveway and we won't make the movie in time!"*

She took a deep breath, untwisted the seatbelt, released it slowly... and BOOM! It worked. Problem solved. She had a giggle in her voice because she was proud that she'd overcome the challenge.

Now, I may sound like a mother torturing her daughter, BUT guess what's never been a problem again? And I've lost COUNT of the number of times I've used that scenario as an example for people being stuck.

Now, confession time! There are MANY times I get stuck, myself. I'm a hyper chick at times with a fiery Croatian nature. When I'm in rage or any kind of extreme emotion, I can't see the wood for the trees!

## YOU ▮

I'm trapped in my shit: trapped, blind, stuck, and frustrated!

I've recently been learning some more spiritual stuff. Lately, I've had to really dig! My friend Nat calls me "Doug" cause I've had to dig deep at times!

The ONE thing that we can ALL do when facing a problem is step back. Physically walk to another space, even just another room, and take three big deep breaths—in through the nose…out through the mouth.

Suddenly—your head becomes clear. You are calmer and can actually see solutions!

It's like those pictures that if you stare at long enough and adjust your eyes, a 3D image pops out at you. It's just a case of switching your perception.

Solutions are sitting there! We just tend to block them with our emotions.

There is nothing wrong with being fiery or frustrated. Embrace that fire if that is part of who you are! In fact, I LOVE that I'm a little fiery. Strong emotions are just opportunities for us to learn to regroup and to train ourselves to snap into a better state faster.

# LadyBalls

So next time you're screaming, "THERE IS NO SOLUTION!" there is...

## Just walk away, take three breaths and look again!

I bet you'll see a solution.

---

**DOWNLOAD THE
"SEAT BELT THEORY" exercise.
It's free over at:
www.ladyballsthebook.com/bonuses**

---

### Yoga Move Through a Shitty Time

HOW THE "STANDING BOW POSE" CAN GET YOU THROUGH WHEN THE SHIT HITS THE FAN!

The shit has hit the fan for me at one point or another in some key areas, especially my health. In fact, all areas EXCEPT my business.

We all get bored sometimes, or lose our mojo. You get so stuck in the crap that it's like you're wading through mud! This goes for relationships that get boring, or breakups, businesses that feel out of whack, those times when you can't be arsed sticking to that fitness regime you set for yourself! We've all been there!

STRAIGHT UP TRUTH: I'm all about being authentic, and I do try to post mostly positive stuff on the ole "FACEPLANT" (that's Facebook) BUT guess what? I'm also all about being authentic, and lately it "ain't all rainbows and butterflies". (*Rocky 5* quote).

I have a rule that I don't share the SHIT stuff on Facebook until I have got past it and can share the strategy as a teaching tool for others.

At one point I had gotten slack in my fitness; my health had taken a massive hit, as had my relationships, and I was paralyzed mentally, and pretty much other than my kids and my business.... everything was a bit fucked!

One night, when I was thinking about my Mac Daddy House and imagining my life in it, and another time while I was getting ready for my upcoming event, I realized that in those moments all the shit I was experiencing went away! I was totally focused and felt great! It was like I was drunk off the vision I have for my future, and in THAT moment, nothing could break me.

# LadyBalls

And that's when it reminded me of yoga! When I was introduced to Bikram Yoga, there was one particular pose I totally buzzed off on. It was the "standing bow pose". And why? With this pose the ONLY way you can actually keep your balance is to stretch your body as far as you possibly can... AND you have to reach FORWARD as far as you possibly can.

It got me thinking that when the shit does hit the fan, (and let's face it, it does from time to time) this pose is the perfect metaphor for life.

When you think your whole world is falling apart, the only way to not fall is to relax...take a deep breath...and push forward.

Visualize the future EXACTLY how you want it to be to the point where it feels real! Jump forward into the future and paint a picture of exactly what you want and then set actions that you can take TODAY to move to-wards that future.

Suddenly you are so inspired by the future you have created for yourself... all the shit falls away... and all you see is greatness ahead of you.

Sure, there are moments when you slip backwards and it's hard to stay focused on the good, but practice. Practice, practice, practice. Train your brain to accept that new normal.

## Relax, breathe and push forward.

### From Overwhelmed to Action

STRAIGHT UP TRUTH: I have hidden in the bathroom for fifteen minutes to take a break from my kids. I have faked a toilet stop to catch my breath. No shit.

At times I thought my head was about to explode.

I felt VERY much like Homer Simpson.

I know some people watch others' Facebook pages and think everything's just fairies and unicorn tea parties. That they have the perfect life and nothing could ever faze them! It's like watching a movie and wishing that was your life, but we all know it's never the full truth!

I'm all about keeping it real! Making sure that I'm being totally authentic and, although, yeah, I do have a pretty sweet life, no matter where you're at, no matter how happy you are, we all get overwhelmed from time to time.

…or ALL the time.

# LadyBalls

I took my three- and five-year-old away on holiday. First time ever. It was so exciting, but for some reason every time I take a trip, the week leading up to it, I seem to overbook myself ridiculously!

Like... really? How the hell would I get it all done?

Then when I think I've taken on too much, I'll just take on some more.

I do work best under pressure, but for some reason I go totally overboard before a trip! Maybe because I have an actual deadline I feel I need to do EVERYTHING!!!!

So here are four ways to snap yourself OUT of being overwhelmed and chill the fuck out!

**1.** *Easy one here.... JUST SAY NO!*

> If people ask you to do something, ask yourself this question: is this opportunity or task moving me towards my goals?
>
> Sometimes what SEEMS like an opportunity can actually be a time sucking nightmare! You don't HAVE to say yes to everyone. Keep things simple!

## YOU ∎

2. *Have an accountability partner who can talk you off a ledge.*

   Have someone you connect with for fifteen minutes each week. You list your top three important tasks for the week, and then have them list theirs. Then, each week you check in on what you achieved, and set up the next week. Then you have someone to answer to.

   That way, when the shit hits the fan (as it always will at some point), you can call this person up and brain dump. Allow them to mentally slap you and get back on your path!

3. *List it out!*

   Brain dump EVERYTHING you have to do, then go back over it and pick the top three things, then get 'em done. Move some things so that they spread out over the next few days and DELEGATE what you can! Rome wasn't built in a day, and it sure as hell wasn't built by ONE man!!

4. *This is the big one.... I'm 97% certain that we're all crazy!! At least at some point! I sure as hell am most of the time.*

   So when you feel yourself go into overwhelm.... go somewhere alone. Take three big really deep breaths and just chill. Zen it out. Take a day off or even just a

# LadyBalls

couple hours for yourself where you have to answer to no one and can just breathe.

## Good shit just happens when you breathe and are in flow.

I swear... it works wonders and will stop you wanting to jump offthenearestbridge.

### Erase The Bullshit That's Stopping You From Smashing Goals

Whether we admit it or not, us humans, we loooooove us some drama! We can take the tiniest little things and turn them into a snowball of crazy overnight.

We're our own worst enemies! But there is one cool little exercise you can do to overcome all that crap in just a few short minutes! And I'm about to tell you how.

I was broke, living on the bones of my ass, hating myself... but what happens next will shock you. (Haha—I've always wanted to say that!)

Let's face it—we're all messed up in some way, shape, or form. And usually it's a result of something big that's happened to us in our past. Well, something that we

## YOU

PERCEIVE as big, because we blew it up into a giant bubble of mentalness!

That's okay! We're all human. It's what we do! The first step is to just own the feelings. If not, then you'll spend your life judging yourself and that will only downward spiral you to the depths of hell.

I'm going to share with you my personal lesson with this exercise.

If you haven't heard my confession before, in my twenties I nearly went bankrupt. Not once, but twice! I was $65k in debt at twenty-five and it did my head in.

Every time I checked the mail, there were bills and debt collection letters up the wazoo, and each envelope had me hating myself a little bit more.

### What a loser! What a fuck up! How did I get myself in this mess?!

I was in the middle of a course and got out a pen and paper and just started writing every single little thing about the debt that came to my head.

# LadyBalls

In doing this writing exercise, I spent ten minutes and I wrote pages and pages of self-loathing, cancerous bullshit. It went on and on and on.

I then took a highlighter, and we had to ONLY highlighted what was FACT. And in all the bullshit I'd been spinning in my head the only FACT was...

When I was twenty-one, I got all the credit cards I could get and set off on an adventure around Europe and overspent on all the cards.

Every other word I wrote was just bullshit! Exaggerated, made up, self-judging bullshit!

> Once you see how much crap you feed your mind and just look at the facts... only THEN can you see a solution to SOLVE the problem.

After that, I got a book that took me through a process to get out of debt, and I followed it, and before you knew it, the debt was gone. What an exhilarating moment it was to know that the debt was gone and that I had the knowledge and the exercises to help me overcome my crap!

### Riding Out the Highs and Lows

Life tends to go through peaks and troughs.

YAY—Everything is going so weeeellll—World domination…

Then….

Boooooo—the shits hit the fan—

## I'm depressed. Kill me now.

Wait… I'm happy again! Yay! I'm amazing!

You know how it goes: everything's going swimmingly, you're in the vibe, you're on a roll. Life could not be better….

…then smack! You get smashed in the face with an emotional brick and your world comes crumbling down.

We all experience it on some level. Some more extremely than others. Myself… I'm extreme. But you know what…. I kinda like it. Keeps things spicy.

# ▌LadyBalls

Now, I'm always talking about embracing who you are, both good and bad, but what happens when you are in that sucky place and you're not taking action in your business, you're feeling resentful, you're sabotaging your relationships, and you're bringing YOURSELF down?!

How can you snap out of it?

Whatever happened to the law of attraction 101? Where everything goes right and stays that way if you're in the vibration? With this law that everyone raves about, there should be no bad when there is so much good, right?

There are three things you need to remember.

1. *BAD SHIT HAPPENS TO GOOD PEOPLE, and it's there to show us contrast.*

Your perception of a situation is never good nor bad until it's compared to another situation. One week might be smooth sailing everything going RIGHT... and THEN the next—everything's turned into a shit sandwich!

But unless you have that contrast, how are we to enjoy the great stuff if we can't compare it to the bad?

**YOU** ■

2. *You can 120% guarantee that after a shit time comes a good time, and vice versa.*

   Waves of awesomeness and waves of crap. Any cool person knows what to do when the waves are pumping....you grab your surfboard and ride that mofo like you OWN it!

3. *It's easier said than done to snap out of a funk....*

   You would have heard this a squillion times, but JUST DO IT! It works. (Credit to *Nike* for reminding us of that constantly.)

## Fortune favors peeps who get shit done.

Trust the process, embrace that life does come in peaks and troughs, or else we'd never learn anything, and we'd remain stagnant and bored out of our brains!

Keep the big picture in focus even at the worst of times and keep on driving.... drive, drive, drive towards it with actions and unwavering faith that everything is just as it should be.

# LadyBalls

When you are there and the emotional bricks come at you again, you can Bruce Lee those bad boys off with ease and grace.

### *3 Ways To Smash Through Your Comfort Zone*

If you watch my shows, then you know I loves me some good ole, fire up, inspiration station, motivation... from any nation.... and I like to rap.

I was slap-me-in-the-face blown away by Felix Baumgartner and his jump from space when he did it. It was all very fitting for what was happening to me at the time.

It's so inspiring watching someone perform an astounding feat...break crazy records that generations before us would have regarded as IMPOSSIBLE...

...and knowing that someone in the future will SMASH THAT record as well.

Humans are forever evolving, improving, and smashing through comfort zones and barriers. Barriers that are put there by humans themselves.

Now, I know you've heard all this before, but we need to be constantly reminded of just how FREAKING AWESOME we humans all are!

## YOU ▌

> We all have an astounding power to take charge of our lives. Not just to survive, but to really kick ass.

I'd been having some huge breakthrough moments. Kind of like I'd been smashing through some limiting beliefs that were holding me back in ALL areas of my life.

On a recent trip to Vegas to hang with my mastermind peeps, I went on the Big Shot drop from the top of the stratosphere. The drop was 1,149 feet up at the top of the tallest building.

Now, I know that's no drop from space, but.... I went on this trip with the intention of breaking out of my comfort zone. I wanted to push myself more than usual to see what I came up with.

For me, doing the drop was something I wouldn't normally do. In fact, it was several potential upchuck situations there. (That's my professional term — yes, you can use it).

But when I did do it, it was like a big 1149 foot metaphor for what was happening on that trip. It was a great

**LadyBalls**

feeling, the whole week was fantastic, and I felt great about where my business was going. How far I'd come and what I had planned for the next 90 days.

HOWEVER TREVOR....it's JUST as easy for us to slip back into our comfort zones. The key is to learn your triggers that snap you out of it so you can start to control them.

Here are 3 tips that I got out of watching the space jump and what's been happening in my life lately.

1. JUST DECIDE whatever it is you want to do... just decide, set a plan, and make it happen. No excuses.

   Set yourself a rule. NO EXCUSES. Make it part of your core values. No whining. No complaining to your friends.

   Whatever you focus on you breed in your mind. If you complain to your friends, then you're creating that energy. If you're going to whine about it... stay on your couch and watch tv, stay broke, and just survive.

## YOU

If you have a picture of your ideal life in your head, be it your business, your health, relationships—work out what you want... and go get it.

2. RESISTANCE IS A BITCH and it will kick you to the ground any opportunity it has. Just when you think you're flying towards your goal, something always seems to pop up and punch you in the face with a king hit.

Deal with it... that's going to happen. ALWAYS. So when it does hit you, be prepared. Know your triggers and Trojan on. Push through, no matter what! Don't let hurdles stop you from achieving.

Just keep going. Keep going and keep going until you nail it. Then nail it better.

## Life is meant to be EXCEPTIONAL. Good is the poor man's great.

3. Finally.... Think about each area of your life. Are they ALL exceptional? When you wake in the morning, do you mentally high-five yourself and say. *"Yeah baby... this is my life...—that's how I roll"*?

**▌LadyBalls**

If you don't, then fix it.

> "On the field of the Self stand a knight and a dragon. You are the knight. Resistance is the dragon."
> **~Steven Pressfield**

If that voice in your head is saying *"easier said than done,"* THAT VOICE IS RESISTANCE. Tell her back the truck up and get outta ya face. You got things to do.

So if you find yourself sitting at your desk going round in circles... Or if you are staring into space wishing life was different... Or if you look in the mirror and you're not happy with your health....

DECIDE... BREAK THROUGH RESISTANCE... and CREATE your EXCEPTIONAL LIFE....

Life is too short not to kick ass!

Resistance can be a sneaky shit. Stay Diligent.

And remember.... if one hundred years ago someone said that one day a man would jump from space to the Earth, they would have been wrapped in some freaky-deaky *Silence of the Lambs* straight-jacket and sent to the loony bin.

You can achieve ANYTHING. Even the stuff you might not believe yet.

NO HOLDS BARRED. NO LIMITS.

You, my friend, are powerful beyond measure.

**What is your body telling you?**

Our bodies are the best communicators. If we are hurt, sick, or injured it's our mind asking our body to grab our attention. Then we can take a look at what is going on and make a change. If we ignore pain or symptoms and drug ourselves numb, then instead of acknowledging the message and working out what's going on, we are depriving ourselves of our best supporter.

I am addicted to kickboxing. A spiritual healer in Bali told me I'm addicted to it because it is my physical way of expressing emotions that I tend to hold inside. It's my outlet for emotional thoughts.

# ▌LadyBalls

I love that.

So I am often getting injured. Not because of getting my ass kicked, but because I may not be executing the technique right. Even then there is a message in it.

For example, when I was doing two minutes hardcore of knees at kickboxing I got tired, and my knee started to drop. When the two minutes were up, I had a massive blue lump on my knee. I'm an all or nothing person, so I kept kneeing through the pain. However, that would never have happened if I was not tired.

The message there was that when we get tired, we tend to try to push through and not focus on the right stuff. It would have been better to do less knees but keep the technique right.

How many times in business do we get burnt out but keep going and then make mistakes? It was not just a message for my body—it was a metaphor for what we action every day in our businesses.

Another time, I was doing hooks. I LOVE hooks. I was going so hard and fast I went into a zone and the punches got stronger and it was euphoric... until I got a massive cramp up my neck. I nearly spewed, it was so painful.

## YOU

The message was that when my Croatian rage kicks in and adrenaline pumps, I lose the hook technique and tense up my shoulders, which caused this injury. Again, a metaphor.

> **If you come from a place that is relaxed and focused, then the result will be far better than if you are go-hard-crazy.**

I have a test that I use to make sure that I am only doing things I love and not things that have me being out of flow. When I'm working on a task, I will check in with my body to see how I am posture-wise and if there is any tension. I carry tension in my shoulders, so as soon as I find myself tight across the back, I will immediate delegate that task.

It's important as an entrepreneur or creator of anything to keep focused on the big picture. Working on things that have us out of flow will hinder our big picture, not move us forward.

Get into the habit of testing yourself. Have your alarm set on your phone to check in every few hours and ask yourself how you feel. Are you inspired, on fire and does time just seems to disappear? OR are you tense, lethargic and time is dragging?

It's pretty basic.

> If it feels good—do it.
> If it doesn't—automate.

If it feels good—do it. If it doesn't—automate or delegate it.

---

**LISTEN TO THE FREE AUDIO**
"What is your body telling you?"
And discover the signals that will have you playing your best game in life.
It's free over at:
www.ladyballsthebook.com/bonuses

## #1 Trick to Kill Self-Doubt

What if I fail?
What if no one likes me?
What if they don't buy my stuff?

Fear not citizens! I have a trick to banish self-doubt forever!

People are always asking me to do videos on mindset, self-doubt, and procrastination. As entrepreneurs, it's not always easy working alone, by yourself.

You quit ya day job with visions of world domination, but next thing you're in your onesies rocking back and forth in the corner wondering how you'll pay ya mortgage.

I know that feeling. I've been there! Seven years ago, I was so close to bankruptcy it wasn't funny!

I was broke, stressed, mentally shattered, and, suddenly, I was also pregnant.

Nothing slaps you to wake the hell up like being responsible for another human!

■ LadyBalls

Why do we need to wait for a shocking life changing circumstance or a near-death experience to get our shit sorted?

Get comfortable with being uncomfortable! Commit to your ultimate life right now!!! Do whatever it takes!

Here's the difference between you making it and being "one of them" statistics.

When you get low, doubt your ability, think who am I to teach this? Why would anyone listen to me? When you just feel it's easier to get a job or go to another motivational seminar searching for that magic bullet...

Remember this: STOP IT! Just stop it!!!

## Sometimes you gotta step up so you don't fall back.

I 100% Guarantee you are better than you think you are. There are people who know you who see your magnificence and if you could see yourself through their eyes, your whole world would open up for you.

Stop living in a glass jar, only ever reaching the lid. Smash that lid off, reach up and grab everything you've

## YOU ∎

ever wanted. It's sitting there waiting for you and it's yours for the taking.

You have to stop the bullshit talk, stop over-analyzing and start executing your plan!

How many times do you hear yourself say *'man, time flies.'* It's another month gone. Next thing you know, you're eighty-five wishing you'd lived more.

The time to rise up and live that life you dream of is now! Wake up! Take responsibility and make it happen!

When you feel yourself slip back (and you will because resistance is a bitch), just cut it out and do one more thing that moves you closer to your goal.

Send out that one blog post or email, test a new Facebook ad or post. Record a video with a tip or strategy. Just take one action—one small step! Even small steps will get you up a mountain if you just keep taking them!

I know this might sound brutal... Everyone's got their bullshit voice in their head: *I was bullied at school, my parents didn't love me enough, my parents loved me too much, I'm shy, I'm introverted...* whatever your story.

# LadyBalls

Leave it at the door. Look at where you are in your life right now and how frustrated you are with your current situation, and ask yourself this...

*"If I stay here in this place and don't step up, what will my life look like in twelve months?"*

Scary huh?

Now, ask yourself this: *"If I DO step up, drop the negative bullshit and take action, do what I know I need to do... What would my life in twelve months be like?"*

Exciting right?

I know this is harsh, but you don't have time to muck around! You've got your big kids pants on now... Wear 'em like you mean it!

## Know in your heart of hearts that your life is changing right now because it is. Just trust the process and keep taking those steps!!!

## YOU

I'm here to support you and kick your ass if you need it.

So go out there, re-adjust those big kid pants and smash it!!!

**Letting Go**

Let go....

Of that THING that's holding you back, of that person pushing your emotional buttons, the excuses that stop you playing the biggest game you can, the self-doubt that has you paralyzed, that thought that you're not enough... 'cause you ARE enough. You're more than enough. You're everything you could possibly need to have, EVERYTHING you want... once you let it all go. Just take a deep breath... and let it go...

I LOVE FEELING SMALL.

We are all so INSIGNIFICANT, yet SO significant.

I may be "out there" and OTT on Facebook (as I am in real life) and l like to socialize and party. I'm opinionated and speak my mind with no filter (despite the shit-storms some of my public outbursts cause).

# LadyBalls

It doesn't take a rocket scientist to see that I have a higher daily word count than most, and that just has to get out of my brain, or I'll internally combust. If you're reading this, then you feel the wrath of my daily rants already!

I was that kid who everyone shot down saying, "*stop trying to always be the center of attention*". I see it now as a POSITIVE trait. If one thing I say out loud improves someone's day, or inspired them, (even if it's just making them laugh AT me), then I've had a positive effect on someone's life, and it makes it all worth it. It's even more fun if it's something that others are afraid of saying.

BUT....

There is nothing more empowering to me than the feeling of being so INSIGNIFICANT!!! Feeling so small that I don't even matter in the grand scheme of things. Those moments when you realize that the universe is fucking infinite!

We get caught up in our small day to day shit that seems sooooo huge to us mentally; the drama that we as humans love to thrive on; that addiction to the drama and to our shit that it holds us back.

## YOU ∎

Dudes walk on the moon, break sound barriers, smash world records that people before believed were impossible....

There are infinite possibilities for EVERYONE to live the life they want and to smash the goals they want to achieve.

Infinity quote???

Just look out at the ocean... look past the horizon... INFINITE. Gaze at the stars tonight, and look past what you see... The UNIVERSE IS LITERALLY INFINITE!

Next time you fly, look out the window at the perspective of the small dots on the world we are in, then see how suddenly the drama and bullshit seems insignificant.

We all need to be reminded from time to time (me included) just how there are UNLIMITED POSSIBILITIES for our lives. Some things we have not even thought of yet!

So think about it now...

What kind of life do you want to live?

What do you want to do with your time?

**▌LadyBalls**

What would it be like to have a business model leveraged and automated so you can live that lifestyle?

If you read this and can FEEL the possibilities that are waiting for you, and you want to talk to me directly on how I can help you do that, then let's jump on the phone together. Let's blow the roof off your dreams and engineer a simple strategy to make that happen.

> **When my son Joey was three, he believed as long as he wore his sisters wings he could safely jump from the top of her bunk. He believed it… so every time… he landed perfectly. Somewhere along the way we develop fears and stop believing. We restrain ourselves with the limitations WE create! Some days we just have to chill out and think like a kid again. LIMITLESS. Find your limitless inner child.**

# 5
# LIFESTYLE BY DESIGN

# LadyBalls

So often people have an idea of what they want, but they never get there. This is usually because they have these invisible barriers stopping them.

*But I'm a mum, dad.*
*But I'm a wife, husband*
*But I don't have the money.*
*But I'm not educated.*
*But I'm not ... [insert bullshit excuse here].*

Or maybe what they want seems so far out of reach they never try to get there.

## 4 steps to getting what you want:

1. *Get really clear on what you want—specifics.* Example: I know the exact sound proofing that will be on the walls of the music room in my "Mac Daddy" house (AKA Dream house).

2. *Go big—don't limit yourself.* After all, this is your ULTIMATE lifestyle, not your half pie lifestyle.

3. *Know your lifestyle number.* List every single thing you can possible want if money and time were no object. Work out how much you need to earn to support that lifestyle.

## Lifestyle by Design ∎

**4.** *Set the actions.* Sometimes getting everything you want is just a case of logistics! You just need a detailed action plan and tick each thing off one by one.

For example, I have designed in my head the most beautiful home that photographers will be begging to use for shoots, that people will be jumping over each other to be married in, and the house magazines will be killing each other to feature this unique property.

It has been a dream of mine since I was fourteen. The house has grown since then with many new features but to make it real I had to break it down into actions.

Find the land. Get the drawings done. Get clear on every detail of the house. I know which sound system will be installed through the entire property and where the second dwelling will be that the house manager will live in full time.

It's all in the details. That's how it moves from an idea and then manifests into reality.

Get yourself a journal. Work out your lifestyle number how much you need and add images in there and specifics of the lifestyle you want.

Whether you are designing your dream home, your ideal relationship, mapping out your business... make a decision to ONLY settle for exceptional.

Don't half-pie it. Have no limits. Go for the absolute ultimate and never sell yourself short.

> That awesome moment when you realize something you love about your life and then suddenly remember you visualized the crap out of it not that long ago but you can't even remember when it switched from just visualizing to reality.

## Entrepreneurs Vortex

HELP! I'm stuck inside a box with NO human contact. It is the vortex of self-destruction.

As creative entrepreneurs, from time to time we are so head-down bum-up working like crazy we don't realize that we've gone days without contact from the outside world.

Sure we have skype videoing, and phone calls all day long... but it doesn't FULLY replace human contact.

## We are not Robots.

I'm not saying that you want to run out and start stroking any human you see in the street to fill your cup of human touch.'

I'm talking about that eye contact, face-to-face interaction... we all need it. From birth, human contact is what forms bonds and somewhere on the net I read (which makes it true by the way) that human connection is the next most important thing for humans after SURVIVAL.

I guess if you haven't got survival nailed you're up shit creek without a paddle.

I admit that there are two sides to me. There is the side of me that likes to socialize, be on a stage, be loud and have loads of fun. BUT... there is also a side of me that craves being a little introverted. I come home from an event and all I want to do is go underground, watch movies in bed, and chill out with my kids.

A lot of us have this, and we should embrace it, and go with it.

■ **LadyBalls**

After about a week of being introverted and hiding from the world... I CRAVE getting out there again! Be it a speaking gig, or a social event, or carving up a dance floor with my helicopter moves where my arms become weapons to poor innocent bystanders.

If I don't get out of my office and go do things like fancy lunches or go to the beach, or party with friends, I go crazy AND it completely stunts my creativity.

One minute you are spewing genius on a whiteboard loving your stuff...next minute you're doubting your abilities and are trying to FORCE your ideas and WILL making money so hard that you are really just banging your head on a wall!

THE SOLUTIONS: Because we're all about solutions 'round here...

1. Embrace that you have changing moods and go with them.
2. If creating or making money feels like hard work... get out of the office... go to lunch, shop, or just get out and walk.
3. Listen to your body. If you are sitting at your desk hunched over and your shoulders are tight, or you have a burning in your gut, it's your body telling you to walk away.

If you apply those three things, then you will have less time trying to force your genius and more time letting your genius flow through you.

> When you're in that flow state it'll be like you're channeling pure brilliance and everything will just seem easier!

## How To Get More Done

Do you find it hard to nail a task because of your lack of focus, or you're getting overwhelmed? Me too.

I'm a VERY easily distracted person. It doesn't take much for me to get distracted.

**I'm going to give you my three strategies for staying focused and smashing out your goals:**

**1.** *Take action in bed before the sun comes up.*

> I know what you were thinking, but it's not that! Well —I guess that can also start your day off happy, so whatever blows your skirt up, love!

# LadyBalls

Seriously though...

I was in Vegas hanging with my Mastermind family and my mentor Kevin Nations said, *"plant a seed every day before the sun comes up"*.

Now I do whatever that genius of a man tells me.

So now, I make sure that before 7 a.m., while I'm still in bed, I take an action that is geared towards meeting my big picture goals. Things like...

- Ask a question to my Facebook peeps to see what kind of cool shit I write about
- Delegate stuff to my House Manager so I have more time to get shit done and hang with my kids and live the dream :)

Do anything the frees up your time or brings in sales.

## 30-Minute Increments

This system is my MOST VALUABLE: Run your day in 30-minute increments.

If I cruise through my day with a big overwhelming list, then I don't get jack shit done.

I take the top three things that must be done that day and are key to achieving my sales goals or serving my clients at the highest level.

Then, I block out the day in chunks of thirty-minute increments. Keep it simple.

I ran my kids' joint birthday party in thirty-minute increments. Cake pickup, catering delivered, bouncy castle erected. People thought I was a freak, but when people rocked up I was sitting there, wine in hand, ready to enjoy the day—and a non-stressed mum makes for happy kids.

## Automate. Delegate. Delete Theory.

This is my ADD theory. No, not attention deficit disorder. (Although that is the reason I created this.)

Take your thirty-minute increments from your diary in the last four weeks and your action list for each day, and ask yourself these three most powerful questions....

1. What on this list can I AUTOMATE? Maybe through an email campaign or templates or some sort of software.

■ LadyBalls

You may think, *"but it takes so much to set up!"* and it might, but once it is, it's done and you'll love it.

2. What can I DELEGATE? Is there someone on your team who can do it, or can you bring in someone?

If that voice in your head says, *"it's faster to do it myself!"* then it's the Death of the Entrepreneur talk and you'll never leverage your business. Let go and delegate that shit!

And the last and BEST...

3. What can you DELETE?

Sometimes we spend so much time keeping busy to feel important and fulfilled that we don't get to live a free and cool lifestyle.

Look at me, everyone! I'm so busy and important!

## Which would you prefer... to be busy? Or out living your life doing cool shit?

## Outsourcing

One of the things I spend a lot of time on up front with my clients is delegation. Sometimes, your ultimate lifestyle is out of reach purely because you need to delegate tasks that are not in your flow. There are many websites where you can find such people.

Nothing drives me more crazy than outsourcing an urgent job and what you get back is so crap a five-year-old could have done a better job.

Websites like *fiverr* and *Upwork* are great but you need a system. Usually, you get what you pay for, BUT! recently I've used plenty of people to help me with ur-gent jobs and they've done a great job!

Marketing stuff, graphics, web design, voice-overs etc.

You have to be careful though.... you can easily get sucked into the shiny object abyss and before you know it, you've wasted two hours looking at videos of puppets and rappers and you get NOTHING done!

So here are three things that you need to know to make sure you get the most out of outsourcing sites and the best quality results:

**▌ LadyBalls**

1. Go in there with a mission. Don't just wander over and have a nosey..... have a specific task that you want done, go and search it, and do not be distracted by the puppets.

2. Each task and person has a rating, so you can see who has been rated highly. Usually next to that, you can also see how many people they've done that task for, so the more that's there with the highest rating, the higher the chance of you getting a really good quality job done!

3. Check their portfolio. Make sure it's of a high standard.

One person's job well done is another person's nightmare. Be prepared, because sometimes things are not as good as you'd like. If you can build a team of contractors long term... it's worth it.

## How a House Manager can make you money

Most of us assume that having a house manager is something straight out of *Fresh Prince of Bel Air* or *Richie Rich*. That having a house manager means you're useless and can't do the job yourself, or that you're a bad parent.

As usual, this is just some crazy expectation that society, relatives, and your parent-guilt brain created as a limiting belief. It's bullshit.

Having a house manager is not snobby. It's bloody efficient.

If your car is broken and needs fixing, you take it to a mechanic, right? If you need your house painted, you know getting a professional is a much better option, right? If you break a bone you go to a doctor, right?

As we talked about, anything that is not in your flow you should outsource so that you can focus on your strengths. When you focus on what you are best at, then you are more efficient, things just fall into place, and you reach your goals faster and with ease.

The easier something is to outsource, the better. And cleaning, organizing the house, doing your washing, folding clothes, running to the dry cleaners, scrubbing your oven, prepping your food snacks for the week so you eat healthy…. all these things can be VERY easily outsourced.

**There are two simple steps to it:**

1. Get over the limiting bullshit that tells you all the reasons you shouldn't have a house manager.
2. Get a house manager.

# ▌ LadyBalls

If you need some statistics to justify the decision, here goes.

I have a house manager for ten hours a week. She does all those things I listed above. She thinks of the things I don't in order to make my life easier.

10 hours costs me $180. As an entrepreneur, 10 hours is a shitload of focused business time where you can be making WAY more than $180 in that 10 hours. If you can't make $180 within 10 hours of focused business creation time, then there's a whole other lot of work that needs to be done in terms of your mindset and marketing skills.

10 hours is a whole day at work for peeps in a day job. Imagine having a spare full day each week to create more income in your business. I'm pretty sure if you woke up on a Monday morning and said to yourself, *"My goal today is... (instead of scrubbing shit from the toilets in the house), I'm going to do one thing that can generate $180."* I KNOW you can do that.

She even does a stock take on my freezer. So many things I purchase get thrown in there, and then I forget and unnecessarily buy more.

She did a freezer list so when it comes to meal times, you can look at the list on the fridge and go, *"Oh look—*

*didn't know we had that!"* It has saved me spending more money on more food I already had and getting creative with the freezer contents that already existed.

To overcome your parent guilt… think of how it would affect your kids if two of those spare ten hours were spent hanging with them instead of vacuuming.

To overcome that lying voice that says, *"but I really enjoy cleaning"*… I call bullshit. I'm pretty certain there are many things you'd rather do with your time than suck up dead flies or be flicked in the face with actual shit when you are scrubbing the toilets like you're digging to China.

## 5 Quick Strategies To Generate Cash Fast And Pay For Your House Manager

To overcome justifying the cost, here are five things you could do with that spare one day a week that can generate far more than $180.

1. Do a last minute Google Hangout, and make an offer at the end that they can't refuse.
2. Do a webinar and record it, so you can send the replay out to everyone afterwards with a fast action offer at the end.

3. Post on your Facebook Page and Profile that you are doing a one-day only offer and it's limited to three people and get on the phone with them.
4. Call up someone who said they were not ready or didn't have the money at the time, and offer them something so powerful they would be crazy to say no.
5. Email your existing clients and offer them and upsell

Remember that whatever you offer needs to take less time than those 10 hours, too. Keep it as leveraged as you possibly can.

So there you have it. By now, you should be able to see a house manager as a moneymaker for you!

Get on all the websites you can offer jobs, put it in the local paper, ask your friends on Facebook, call up anyone you think might need to make extra money. My house manager is the daughter of my previous cleaner. I started writing on the fridge under the title HOUSE MANAGER all the things I didn't want to do one week.

My cleaner told me that she knew someone who would do all of those things for me and clean. It worked out.

BOOM! Win!

**Lifestyle by Design**

## Parenting & Biz Juggle

*How not to knock someone's head off during childbirth*

I thought I'd be one of those mums (if I ever had kids) that would have a doctor by the throat begging him for every drug there could be. I was wrong.

I had a dream when I was about three months preggers that there were lily pads all over the Auckland Harbour. People were trying to balance on them and were sinking. I asked the master what they were doing and he said, *"if you can learn to control your mind, you will stand balanced and floating on the lily pad. If you can't master your mind—you sink."*

> "Your pain is the breaking of the shell that encloses your understanding"
> ~Khalil Gibran

I gave it a crack and eventually mastered it and peacefully (and proudly) balanced on the lily pad.

That morning I woke up and opened the local paper. Now, I never watched the news or read the paper, so

# LadyBalls

this was a rare thing for me to do. I opened it up to a random page in the middle and there was an article on Hypnobirthing. It pretty much described a way of birthing that was exactly like the dream I'd had that night.

I immediately called up my man at the time and TOLD him—*This is what I'm doing*. Of course, he thought I was nuts. He knew me more than anyone else, and I'm certain he was rolling his eyeballs thinking, "*oh God—what is she fucking on about now? Her crazy woo woo shit...*". He agreed, though. He knew that was the safe option. :)

We did two classes to learn the technique. It was firstly learning how the body works and that we were designed to birth babies. Once you understand the way the body works you can work with it to have the smoothest birth possible.

The basic premise is that in traumatic situations our bodies choose freeze, fight, or flight. If you freak out, then the body will tense up and not use the functions we were designed with. Now this is clearly easier said than done, so there were breathing techniques and an affirmation and visualization audio I listened to every night for six months.

People say, "*you were so lucky with your births*," but in reality I had to listen and practice every single day until

## Lifestyle by Design

it became so ingrained in me that when it came to the big day it was like second nature. It also involved a lot of NLP so there were certain words that you left out of your vocab, like "pain" and "push" etc. Instead, you "breathe the baby down".

I had Milly in a drug-free birthing center up north in the bush, and I had Joey on the couch at home (on purpose). Both births took around four and a half hours and were EXACTLY as I had visualized them.

After learning that I was capable of training my mind and body to get through that, I thought to myself.... *"If I can do that—what else can I do?"*

I hated long distance running. I was always a sprinter, a short-sharp-bursts girl. So naturally, I thought I'd test myself out and do a half marathon eight months after having my first baby.

I did it! My time was terrible, but I did it! I hardly trained either (cause I like to just totally wreck my body haha). I did another one and took thirty minutes off my previous time.

So after doing the half marathons, I said to myself.... *"If I can do that... what else can I do?"*

■ LadyBalls

I now ask myself that question all the time and constantly uplevel my impossibles to "Nailed it"!

As a result of learning that hypnobirthing technique, it not only gave me the juice to always push myself further than I can imagine, but it also gave me breathing strategies that help with everything. I get the kids to use it when they are constipated, haha. I use it to get through pain, and I see the kids copying that, too. I even use it to get to sleep if I'm struggling.

> We are all capable of so much more than we can even fathom. Pick something impossible and make it your new reality.

## Parent guilt

I only had four days off work when I had my daughter. It was the catalyst for becoming the master of automation, delegation and scalability that I am today.

I felt guilty that I had to work. Guilty that I didn't have enough time for her. Guilty for not being able to breastfeed her. Guilty that I couldn't seem to get that "feed, wind and sleep" around the right way. I couldn't even tell you now which is the "right" way.

## Lifestyle by Design

The worst guilt is when other people rock up and give their "advice", which as a full-of-guilt-mum all you hear is, *"you're doing a shit job and here is how I think you can do better."*

The first three years are the hardest but I found it got way easier... well right up until I decided to go it alone and became a single mum.

They were just turning three and five, and I thought being the "fun mum" as I always was, would work fine. HELL NO! When you go it alone, you lose the balance of the two parents' skills. You may not have agreed on how to parent, but there was some sort of system. Going it alone was like starting all over again.

Fun Mum is great, but there still needs to be boundaries. We lost all boundaries and I would spoil them out of guilt for "breaking the family unit" as everyone seemed to be calling it. There was this whole new mummy guilt and this one sucked ass!

Luckily for the kids, Dad and I had been friends since *we* were kids, and together for a lot of those years, so we agreed to put the kids first. We always had a great system and no drama. However, doing it alone was still tough.

## LadyBalls

There were days they would not listen to me, and I'd hide in the pantry crying, hoping they wouldn't see me. I didn't want to have them see that I felt like a failure as a parent. I used to lock the bathroom door and take fake shits just to get time to hide and cry.

Most the time it was fine, but when it got hard I would hear that evil voice say, *"how am I ever going to do this on my own?"*

As with everything, it got easier. We got some reward systems in place and I learned that yelling made things worse. Now my kids are like a freaking dream most the time. It seems so easy!

But the big thing about parent guilt... it does not serve you. You can't think of solutions when you are stuck in guilt mode. It doesn't help you or your kids. You will forever be stuck on the cycle of guilt and from there you will be trapped and not able to move forward.

When you find yourself feeling the wrath of parent guilt, you have to switch your mindset and remember everything is perfect as it is. When you step back and let the guilt go and take a calm approach, you will see solutions.

Trust the process and know that there is always a light at the end of the tunnel, even if you can't see it yet. Let go of the guilt… and breathe through it.

I find my kids doing video blogs on my phone, drawing little sales funnels, and I see their entrepreneurial skills developing every day. It makes me proud that they watch and learn from me.

It also makes me aware that they pick up SO much more than we realize, so it's important to think of who you want your kids to be when it comes to who YOU are being.

Being a parent is the most challenging job you'll ever have, but it is also the most rewarding. There is nothing that feels better than the unconditional reciprocal love that you and your kids have for each other. It just gets better and better.

■ LadyBalls

> Parenting for the first few years feels like a computer game... you are trying to master a level and just as you do, you shift up to a harder level.... but in the end you nail it and you're like...

**"Yelly" Parent**

With school holidays and trying to run your biz with the kids around, it can get a litt le frustrating. Even though they are a good age to just do their own thing. 100% of the time they refl ect your mood.

It can get very easy to be the yelly parent. However...

I fi nd my kids are the best behaved when I'm the opposite of that. Spend your focused time working and pre-agree that you'll give them a window to do epic shit in the afternoon.

One week, I took them to *Chipmunks* while I wrote more for my book. Another day, *Inflatable World*. The next, while Joey was strawberry-picking, I took Milly to *Toyworld* to buy a toy she's wanted for a long time.

## Lifestyle by Design

The result... My kids were freaking awesome during the holidays, despite a couple of spaz-outs from me while trying to do biz calls. They were playing well together, even saying the sweetest things to each other.

One night out of the blue they came and said: *"You are the best mum in the whole world. It's never boring with you. You buy us stuff and take us to do fun things. It makes us be good."*

One time I thanked them for being so well behaved at an outing and Milly said: *"The reason we are good is you are not always telling us we can't do stuff . You don't say no all the time and you don't say you can't do this 'n that."*

Don't get me wrong... I'm not saying this to brag... We have days where there's yelling and tears (often mine)...

Data proves that if I communicate structured time for work with a promise of playtime and attention, it works a treat. Plus, they mirror your vibe, so keep your shit cool and happy and they will be too!

Lately I've also discovered the power of one hour one-on-one times with each kids. Such a great bonding time is just giving them that one fully focused hour. And it's nice because they hold your hand that whole hour and communicate really important stuff to you.

■ LadyBalls

This is a far cry from when I used to lock myself in the pantry cupboard and cry about how I would survive solo-parenting or take a fake shit to escape!

---

**Download the 5 strategies to have harmonious parenting moments that allow more flow in your business.
It's free over at:
www.ladyballsthebook.com/bonuses**

# 6
# BIZNIZ TIME

■ LadyBalls

## From No List to 5 Figure Days

When I handed my web design company over to the team, I was finally committing and going all-in on mentoring. I had no list, no following, and was starting from scratch.

It took twenty-one days to get the program idea out of my head and onto paper and make my first two sales (both in the same day). I made $16k that day.

I had no money to invest, so I did it all myself. (Now, had I delegated it, I would have made those sales in the first week and probably twice as many!)

That's an example of how you can go from nothing to generating sizable income fairly quickly.

Within ninety days I was doing 5 figure days. I had one simple funnel, and I was video blogging weekly! That was it!

## The Internet = Opportunity.

The Internet has provided us with the perfect platform to get our genius out to the world.

## Bizniz Time

Everything you need to smash your entrepreneurship goals out of the park is right at your fingertips. It gives you the opportunity to go global. There is no need to keep small in your hometown or even country. There is an entire planet of people, and in it is your target marketing just dying to get their hands on your wisdom.

All you have to do is create an irresistible offer, build trust by being authentic and delivering useful content, and then make the actual sale!

Facebook is literally an online worldwide relationship builder. It's not just to share cute cat pics and jokes with your mates. Have you talked to someone on Facebook, then met him or her in real life and felt like you already know them? It's powerful!

You do need to go all in though. You can't just dip your toe in. You have to be mentally committed 100%. There is always some work involved to get set up, so you have to be willing to do the work. That may mean some super long hours to start, but if you're doing something that you are truly passionate about, you will wake up each day amping to get stuck into your venture, boots 'n all!

And once you have set yourself up, if you do it right (focusing on leveraging your time and scalability), then you have set yourself up for your ultimate future where you will work less and have more fun doing it.

That excites me—helping clients define their ultimate life and execute it through Biz

## Your Non-Biz Product Is Valuable

Thinking that because your service is not something that creates profits, it's a harder service to sell?

*Na ah buddy*! Not true! Maybe you're in personal development, health, fitness, etc., your stuff is SUPER VALUABLE.

And I'll prove it to you!

When people teach something like marketing or sales funnels, like I do, then it's really easy for us to prove that there's a return on investment from what we do. You can use stats and case studies of clients to prove your stuff works, as well.

If you sell something that is valid learning, BUT doesn't necessarily provide the client with a profit in return, then it's easy to have the mindset that it's a harder sell.

The truth is though... everyone has a pain that they want fixed! It can be anything in their life or business. Relationships, health, business, mindset, fashion... not just money! In fact the NON-money factors are even more important. Bad relationships can throw your mojo out. Without your health, you're screwed! Nothing will send you broke more than the distraction of a break up or being so sick you can't work.

The key is to determine these 4 steps of the "fixing" process....

1. What is their big-ass pain that they need fixed?

2. How badly is it affecting their lives? You gotta dig deep on that one and really get how it's affecting them emotionally.

■ LadyBalls

3. You need to get them to see what their life, biz, relationships, etc., can be like if they follow a path (that's YOUR path). Paint them a picture.

4. You need to show them that YOU are the person to help them get to that new place.

Now, a massive portion of my clients are Personal Development and Health Coaches of some kind. Technically, they are not a return on investment type product, BUT their new clients have got some massive pain in their lives.

Take a failing marriage, for example. When you're entire relationship is turned upside down and possibly going to end, you're not going to give a shit about money... you're just going to want to find some way to fix the massive void in you that is tearing your life apart.

If you have a formula to help someone through that process, and they are in enough pain to be begging for a solution, then they will pay whatever it takes to get out of the state they are in.

Same goes for health.

## Bizniz Time

# If someone is told they will die in six months if they don't stop smoking, they won't give two shits about money... they just don't want to die!

A powerful question to ask yourself is this: If someone was to follow your formula and do EVERYTHING you told them to, and they got the desired result...

...then, a year later, if you were to ask them what they thought it's worth, they will say a WHOLE lot more than what they'd paid, I bet.

I've seen personal development clients of mine create such life-changing breakthroughs with their clients that those clients would have paid TEN TIMES the amount they did to get the result they got.

So, next time you are doubting your value to the world, or undercharging because you have a perception that a non ROI product is not as valuable, think again. Think of that husband and wife who are in hell and just want it fixed, or the dying dude who just wants to live.

Ask yourself what is the transformation you can cause in their lives that will make their problem better? Your stuff is gold to someone! You just have to establish WHO that someone is, and then market where they hang out!

## Copying Other People's Shit

Have you ever had someone completely rip off your stuff?

OR have you found yourself struggling to find your own voice because you LOVE what someone else is doing and are magnetically following their path?

You could be ripping off other people's shit yourself and not even realize it because you do it subconsciously! BUT here I'll show you what it really means, and it's not that you're a copycat or bad person, deliberately ripping off other people, either.

What seems to happen, though, is that so many people doubt themselves and their abilities, that next thing you know they are accidentally or subconsciously copying someone they admire.

And I'm not just talking websites here! I mean changing their business to deliver the same stuff as their idol!

**Bizniz Time**

Most people don't do it deliberately, and they may not even be aware that they are doing it!

Now, I let people use the same website theme as me. And there are a couple of scripts in the sales process I GIVE to my clients. Not ALL, but a few for them to model off of. But when I see someone copying fine details of my stuff and their videos are so close to mine that I get private messages from people pointing it out.... I just feel bad for them. Here's why...

> Copying someone else's stuff screams one thing.... YOU DON'T BACK YOURSELF ENOUGH TO DELIVER YOUR OWN MAGIC IN YOUR OWN UNIQUE WAY!

It's got insecurity written all over it. That's why I don't get MAD when people copy me. Personally... I just feel bad for them.

I want everyone to find their own voice and shine their own light on the world. There is no need to lack confidence in what you do. We are all still learning.

▌ LadyBalls

> We are always growing and are never constant. Even the most famous and successful teachers are still on their way.

There is a difference between collating the best of the best and blatant copying too. I mean, look at personal development coaches. They are preaching the same stuff that leaders before us have—Presidents and even mathematicians from years ago.

BUT the GOOD ones will put their own spin and their own personality into it.

Most of us people in Internet Marketing are preaching the same stuff , BUT we all have SOMETHING that we excel at. Find what YOUR superpower is. And then with YOUR personality and YOUR voice, spread that to the world.

Watch how the karma of being true to yourself and truly serving others brings you in all the money and happiness you need.

If your biz feels like hard work, maybe you haven't found that superpower yet. Ask yourself deeply....

Bizniz Time ∎

> What do you LOVE? What makes you HAPPY!? Then go out and monetize that shit!

**Smashing Your Money Blocks**

> Scared that if you raise your prices no one will buy your stuff? Don't worry—that's just your self-doubt and resistance messing with your head.

It's a false belief. It's a trick. Raise your prices and step up to your new normal. Let's face it... everyone is full of self-doubt. It's just that some people know how to handle their negative mind tricks faster than others.

Most people are also charging crazy low prices because they are undervaluing themselves and don't think people will buy.

Almost all my clients come to me undercharging, and we smash that limiting belief out of the water. Then, we build them a kick ass sales funnel to sell their shit, and prove that evil little voice in their head WRONG.

■ LadyBalls

I'll give you an example of a client:

### Phase 1—The Comfort Zone
A client is charging $80 per hour. They are great at what they do but undervaluing it by charging low.

### Phase 2—The Decision.
They realize they are undervaluing and never going to grow their business, so they decide to make a change.

### Phase 3—STRETCH
We create an offer that is mainly video-based and leveraged and is 12 weeks for $4,500. This is way outside their comfort zone. They want to flick back to the "safe" place but instead they push through.

### Phase 4—S.Y.S.
That stands for *Shit Your Self*. This is when my client is just about to break through the terror barrier and switching that paradigm permanently to the final phase.

### Phase 5—Hitting the Terror Barrier
The client has stretched so far out of their comfort zone and are freaking out! They are dying to shrink back, but they gave that barrier a good nudge with their head. It doesn't crack.

They make their first sale at the new price. They think it's a mistake. Who would pay them that?

Did they fall on the keyboard by accident?

Then the second person buys. And that is when we hit....

**Phase 6 — The New Normal**
This is FREEDOM baby. After this, you will never shrink back again! You are free!

And the beauty of this 6-phase trip is that you can apply it to ANYTHING that you fear.

Relationships, business, raising prices, making a big decision.... anything.

---

**WATCH THE FREE VIDEO
"TERROR BARRIER"
It's free over at:
www.ladyballsthebook.com/bonuses**

■ LadyBalls

## Tsunami of Leads And Momentum

WARNING: You are about to experience the TSUNAMI OF AWESOME.

Red light days: when everything turns to shit—ya stub ya toe, break a nail, internet's down, and you seem to catch every red traffic light there is.

Green light days: those days when everything flooooows. You're on time, you make epic sales, everything's going swimmingly, and you seem to catch ONLY green lights.

**This is a formula for momentum, so you can have everything FLOOOOOWWWWW and go EXACTLY how you want and ditch those days where everything's just one giant clusterfuck.**

When I first started video blogging, it was pretty much the only strategy I had out there to generate leads. They were simple short sharp videos BUT the fan-following picked up each week. In fact, the amount of viewers pretty much doubled every video.

**Bizniz Time**

## Blogging is not article writing. Think of it more as powerful brain farts. Short. To the point. With an action.

I had no list, no followers. Within ninety days, I was getting 5-figure sales days from those videos. I was pretty stoked with myself.

Now, I'm not saying this to brag, and I cannot guarantee that EVERYONE will get that, although you totally can... in fact, I invite you to kick my ass at it and we'll celebrate together!

The pattern of the blog growing exponentially is true.... now my numbers are way bigger these days in both leads and sales.

At one point, I broke my rule and was only video blogging monthly, not weekly, and guess what?

I'd built up the magic M-word, so it didn't affect anything. The M-word... MOMENTUM.

BUT then I messed up royally!

**LadyBalls**

I went underground waaaaaaaaay too long. I took my eye off the ball to renovate a house and didn't blog for months! I got nasty emails from people who relied on my videos to keep them fired up and they were PISSED!

## WHY HAVEN'T YOU BLOGGED. I NEED THOSE VIDEOS!

I certainly wouldn't take on clients like that, but you get my point.

Once I started videoing again, I'd LOST so much momentum that it was almost like starting over. It took a couple of weeks, but the leads started to flow back in again.

PLUS... once you're used to it... doing videos like this is soooooo much fun!!!

So THAT is when I defined my 3-part formula for Momentum! Here it is.... (ignore what you learned in school)

# 7

## CONSISTENCY

■ LadyBalls

**...O**r as I prefer to call it: THE TSUNAMI OF AWESOME. NOW.... let's break it down.

## Consistency

As I pointed out, you need to be consistent. Weekly is great for blogging. I like Fridays at 3pm because people are over their week and looking for distraction and searching for ways to change their life if they've had a shit week. So end of business day Friday is perfect.

## Authenticity

You know this is my thing. Don't try fit a square peg in a round hole. BE YOURSELF. That's the guaranteed way to be unique and stand out AND only attract clients you truly resonate with. It's so much more fun to have clients you'd love to hang out with.

## Time

Of course do those two things over time, delivering great content, and you, my friend, are golden.

So.... crank out four blog post scripts this week. Hook up your phone or video gears and get filming...

Blogging will be one of the most cost effective and client-getting strategies you'll ever do and it gives the world a chance to really get to know YOU!

Don't hide, stand tall, and shine like a freakin disco ball, my friends. Because YOUR peeps... will LOVE YOU.

## 3-point Check Of A Well-Oiled Sales Funnel

*No ones watching my videos?*
*My ads won't get approved.*
*WHY no clicks?*
*I need conversion!*
*Where are all the sales?*

Aaaaaagggggghhhh! If I want something, I want it right away. My staff used to call me Veruca. Remember the little girl out of Charlie and the Chocolate Factory? The one who wanted everything RIGHT NOW!

Sometimes, when we set up a sales funnel in our business, we want to get sales immediately.

The sales funnel that has always worked for me is actually pretty simple, but there are some components to it, and what might work for some may need tweaking in a different industry.

■ LadyBalls

Think of your funnel as a well-oiled machine. A machine has multiple moving parts. Just like a vehicle: you can set up an engine, but if one part is out of place, the whole thing won't work.

This is the same for sales funnels.

However.... the thing to remember is that a funnel is pretty basic. You feed traffic to a place where you deliver content to warm them up, and then once they're warm, you offer them something to buy.

This system has worked for many people for many years.

The key is tweaking the machine until it's working smoothly. Don't freak out on day one when you didn't make a million bucks. Just trust the process... tweak your funnel.... watch your Google stats and your opt-in rates or video watch rates and see where the machine is not working... then fix it!

It really is that easy!

## Consistency

We all want it right now! BUT... just trust the process, find the problem, and apply a solution. Keep calm, and if you can't get it to work, seek help from a professional.

An Internet Marketing professional, not a mental institute. :)

## 3 Program Ideas

Tell me if this sounds like you.....

You have a skill or knowledge that you know people can use to improve their life or business, but you feel trapped, overwhelmed, and probably want more cash! You're already teaching your stuff, maybe to your clients one-on-one, maybe it's something you're already doing in your day job! BUT you know it's not scalable. If you were to double your client base tomorrow or work twice as hard at your job... you'd have no time left to sleep, eat or live?

In fact, you probably feel like that right now. You're working your ass off sharing great stuff, but you're stuck...

You're capped at the income you earn because you just don't have the time to increase your hours or clients.... at least not without never seeing your friends or family ever again.

# LadyBalls

Mentally, you're drained because you're not moving forward financially and therefore you're stripping yourself of the lifestyle you want and deserve!

I get it! I've been there! That feeling when you're sitting at your desk, shoulders tense... thinking... I'm never going to get this all done today!

> If you feel like you're on that brutal treadmill, not moving forward, not stepping up, then check this out...

I'm going to share with you my simple BOOM! Funnel that once applied is a well-oiled business machine to get you loyal fans and epic profits. It's the exact model I use myself!

You'll see how you can gain back your freedom to do the things you want that somewhere along the path got lost, like spending time with the family, taking those trips you've been putting off, or just doing epic shit whenever you want!

I love it when people say what's your big picture plan and I can genuinely say... I'm living it!

Consistency ∎

## Business Model Blueprint

YOU are about to see the Business Model Blueprint that only my paying clients have seen. It's a simple 3-step funnel that moves cold leads through a well-oiled business machine. This is the EXACT system that I use to get every single one of my clients, and I have clients doing tens of thousands of dollars in sales a WEEK using this exact funnel.

Now, I don't wanna shock you. This is not complicated. It's not rocket science either....

If you're like me, you want to get from A to B in the shortest possible time. I know it's easy to get overwhelmed and distracted by shiny objects. I mean come on... what fi red up entrepreneur isn't slightly ADD or bipolar, right?

...and have that crazy voice of self-doubt we have to beat down daily!

*Who said that?*

> When you're doing the day-to-day stuff, you're so IN it you can't see the big picture.... it's hard to see the label from inside the bottle.

■ LadyBalls

First, you have to have a funnel. This is the part where people who don't know you from a bar of soap will warm up to you.... they'll see that you know what you're talking about, and they'll resonate with you. (Or they won't but that's okay, too!) When you deliver great content, you build a following of loyal fans who will follow everything you do... and they will buy your stuff!

A funnel on its own will build your list... but you have to funnel them through to somewhere... this is where you send them to a sales page where they can actually BUY from you.

Once they're all warmed up... BOOM! They're ready to take the next step with you, but only after you've shown them that you can help them.

Now with that funnel in place, it's like a shop in the desert... UNLESS you feed that funnel....There are many ways we can do that. Facebook ads, your list, video blogging (which I cover in one of my videos), etc.

It's as simple as that! Build the funnel.... have somewhere they can buy from.... and feed that funnel like the profit machine it is!

## Consistency

It's a simple system that I see work all the time—for me, my clients, and for people all over the world.

Think of the funnel as a machine with some great big cogs: there are the 3 key cogs and there are a series of smaller cogs within these that I teach in my BOOM! program. When they are all working, you have yourself a profit machine that will give you everything you want!

Now, I know they say money can't buy you happiness... but those people just don't know where to shop!

I'm kidding... but I like to think of money as a measuring stick, a reward for providing a service that is helping improve the lives of others, and it just happens to give you the freedom of time if you do it right!

Now, I KNOW you're smart (or you wouldn't be here). So…. I'm not going to go through your "perfect day", or help you work out your big picture goals, or ask if you had all the time and money in the world what would you do. You've probably been through those exercises 1000 times. I agree, they're important, but that is not what this book is about.

■ LadyBalls

> It's about getting stuck in… writing a step-by-step plan…. Then, then executing it. One foot in front of the other. Being responsible for your own actions. This is not hopes and dreams stuff. It's not rainbows and butterflies fluff!

I'm also not the only one out there preaching this stuff. Many other experts or gurus share a similar model. But I am going to do my best to make this the most fun!

Now, let's quickly talk about the big P-word: Profit.

I've created a profit calculator where you can enter your annual money goal and the price of your program, and see how much traffic you need to drive to achieve your goal. http://www.boomformula.com/profitcalc/

---

**Download a more detailed BUSINESS MODEL BLUEPRINT
It's free over at:
www.ladyballsthebook.com/bonuses**

---

## Program structure

Now, I'm all about the leverage. Working less, making more, and having more free time. So that's exactly what you'll be getting from this section. You'll learn three ways to package your genius into programs that are incredibly valuable AND allow you to have enough time to live that lifestyle you dream of.

At this point, don't worry about the detailed levels of your content. If you decide to work with me, we'll work together in detail on that stuff. Right now, you only need to know the result you want your clients to get from working with you.

So consider this....

Imagine someone has worked with you. Zoom forward a year.... they've applied everything you taught them. What do you want them to say was their biggest take away? What result do you want for your clients?

Now, imagine that your program delivers that exact same result.

■ LadyBalls

**Here are 3 Program Structures you can use to teach your content:**

1. Use an online program. Usually a lot of the stuff we teach we find ourselves repeating. If this is the case for you, then you can video record that content and create downloadable workbooks for your clients and they can go through the entire program online without needing you. BOOM! Leverage! You're still teaching the same wisdom... just in a new format.

   It doesn't require you, because the sales funnel to that program is automated, AND you can spend your time just feeding the funnel, or living the dream :0 Whatever that is for you.

2. This is a more interactive version of the previous program: as well as giving access to the step-by-step video system, you can support them in a leveraged way with weekly group calls with you, or by building a supportive community within a private Facebook group.

   Everyone likes to be a part of a supportive community of like-minded people. So create that space for them. They don't need to be face-to-face, and they can chat daily with others on the same journey! They also get access to you, but it's at a structured time

## Consistency

and in a group situation which provides the opportunity for your clients to grow together.

Often when one person asks a question on a group call, a penny drops for another client who's listening in. A group call is a hugely successful way of staying leveraged while providing a massive supportive network for your clients.

**3.** Make a Mastermind group! This is more hands-on and clients have more access to you, BUT they are paying you at a higher premium.

Imagine a group of people working with you over 3, 6, or 12 months. A group of cool people who you work with online in a group scenario, but then every 30-90 days or so you meet up face-to-face and work in a hub of genius, helping them with whatever they need help with at the time. There are less people in the group, but they are paying you more and have direct access to you to fast track them to the next level.

These people are the go-getters. The Mastermind people are your clients who you LOVE working with. You pick and choose who you have in your group because you only want to work with people who get shit done.

■ LadyBalls

People who will apply what you teach them and see the biggest results!

These are my favourite clients to work with. They're clients who you enjoy working with because they are ready and willing to do the work.

**Working with action-takers who apply what you teach will not only get them results, but boost your confidence in what you do. It is proof that you know what you are doing, so those self-doubt days will diminish and you will be empowered to get your genius to more people who need it.**

### 3 Low-Hanging Fruit Strategies

Funnels, opt-ins, sales page, strategy calls, metrics, conversion rates, engagement....

It's no wonder most people get so overwhelmed with all the techy crap and online strategy stuff.

Now, even though I'm the funnel loverrrrrr, and we build these important automated funnels for clients,

## Consistency

I'm going to tell you 3 LOW HANGING FRUIT strategies to bring in sales right away.

There can be a lot of detail in an online funnel, but while that is being built, or ticking over in the background getting you leads, don't underestimate the power of a few simple strategies which I call the GET MONEY NOW strategy.

1. The simple email to your list. This used to be a one-liner email you see a lot now, but I do about three lines so they're a little more qualified. (I got a couple clients to do this in the last week and they got a bunch of responses immediately.)

2. Just ask! If you don't have a list, look on Facebook for some people or maybe some old clients you can upsell. Write a list of 10 peeps you can contact.

This may sound like it goes against my ATTRACT, DON'T DESPERATELY SEEK theory, but it's different because you don't go for the juggular and say BUY MY SHIT MAN—YOU NEED IT! You just start a conversation with them, and ask them where they're at. Find out what their big void is. What is it that is sucking for them right now? See if it's a void you can fill with a hot solution!

I know, it can seem like an old *Amway MLM* move but hey! You're not shoving products down their throats... you're just chatting!

> You don't need to sell. You're just sharing an opportunity and how it will improve their life.

3. Ask the Oracle on FB! If you already have some peeps on Facebook on your page or profile... put up a post saying what the common stress or pain is for your ideal avatar and how you have a solution that may help to solve it. Tell them to private message you if they want to chat about it.

Keep it all simple and conversational. You don't need to hard sell... just chat and be cool.

(#3 on 'roids! Do that as a post on your page, then run a cheap FB ad to the post or boost it!)

BOOM!

You could have several clients sitting right under your nose and all you had to do was ask!

## Consistency

# Get Ideal Clients Falling Into Your Lap

Why haven't they clicked BUY, yet? I talked to them. Maybe I did something wrong? Why do they hate me?

Maybe I should give them a call? Or email them? Or show up at their house? Tap on their window while they sleep?

Creeeeeepppyyy.

I'm kidding, but I am going to tell you why I NEVER follow up a lead and how to just let the ideal clients fall in your lap!

Here are two scenarios... have a think about which you'd prefer. They're true stories, too.

### *Scenario 1:*

Fifteen years ago in London, when I started my first Internet business, I would get a lead. I would then spend an hour on the tube getting to them, sit with them for 60-90 minutes, then tube home for an hour, then quote the job (which even with my templates set up took another hour).

Now work it out. That is…

# LadyBalls

50 billion hours (okay, 4-5 hours) just to quote a client I may never actually get.

Can you imagine the amount of energy that sucked out of me? If I quoted 5 clients a week—that's over 20 hours of chasing leads! Some were not even hot leads.

My close rate was around 60%, so you're talking a full freakin day wasted every week on chasing leads.

And being the dumb ass I was... I would do follow up calls to see if they wanted to be my clients.

PICK ME, PICK ME!

It's like desperately seeking Susan. That's enough cowering to crush Arnie's ego. Just saying.

Telling that story makes me cringe. Fast forward to nowadays....

### Scenario 2:

You build a funnel with shit-hot content...use your list and Facebook ads to drive people there. Other people who like your shit share it, everything's all automated once it's set up, and then it's a just a numbers game.

## Consistency

I get to just hang out living the dream until my team says BOOM! You just made a sale.

For me, the best part is that I get to teach those people who paid me money to do the same thing!

I've got funnels that are so automated you don't do a thing except hang out on Facebook, speaking the truth, go out and play, until a new client comes along. Then I show them how to do it!

I love how in my "job" it's my responsibility to live the freakin dream and teach others to do the same!

One of the highest values in my business is authenticity. Just being myself—putting out the absolute best content and sending those leads, hot or cold, through an online funnel.

Clients have gone through a process before they even speak with a human.

> **The qualifying process is a crucial step in the funnel.**

■ **LadyBalls**

There is no point getting on a phone call with a person who is CLEARLY not a good fit. OR you may as well be sitting on the tube for hours, writing up quotes for hours, and pretty much just wanting to shoot yourself in the face.

Here is the MASSIVE distinction between those two extreme, but true, stories....

The first—you are busting your ass trying to beg someone to become your client.

The second—you are just putting it out there and letting the Universe, the Gods, and plain good ole business karma serve you up with ONLY the coolest clients.

Which would you prefer? Hard work or Easy Street?

Now, even with the funnels if you don't do it right, you could spend a shit ton of time on the phone with un-qualifi ed leads. That's not cool.

So, when you are putting out your content, remember these 3 things:
1. Know who your ideal client is before you create content, and keep that person in mind when you do it.

## Consistency

One of the BEST things I ever did in my funnel was to drop the fluffy shit. None of the "COME ON, YOU CAN DO IT". The people who had to be talked off a ledge every five minutes are not ideal clients.

I went straight for the jugular... METRIX straight up —*"Here are some business offer ideas that are leveraged. And here is a blueprint for how to feed clients to those offers. Want me to help ya? Fill out this qualifying form to see if you're a fit!"*

2. Automate every part of the process you can, and get them to jump through hoops before they get to speak with you.

3. This is THE most important thing: Put your best shit into your content. Always make sure that every bit of content is structured in a way that gets them to ask themselves some hard questions and makes them see the holes in their own business or life.

When they see where they have a void... they know you can help fix it.

Think about how much time you waste talking to non-qualified leads. Or what you can put in place to have the leads begging to be your client as opposed to you chasing them like a desperate little puppy dying for some love.

## Tricks To Avoid Toxic Clients

Toxic clients. Those awful ones that sneak past the qualifying process and ruin your life.

*How the fuck did that one get through?*
*What did I do to attract this?*
*Am I not good at what I do anymore?*
*Do I refund them and move on with my life?*

I'm going to show you how to work out your ideal client and not let the bad apples through, so you can LOVE what you do.

With clients, as with all people in our lives, you want to surround yourself with people who are a joy to be with. Someone you can help to grow, and naturally, you grow in return.

But now and then, somehow, we allow some not-ideals to come into our business space, and it can seriously mess you up! It can leave you doubting your abilities and hating your business. You could have started out loving what you do, and then the odd bad apple ruins that for you.

## Consistency

# Your mind is tricked into thinking you don't love what you do anymore and that you want to throw in the towel.

It can make you think you suck and it makes you blind to the rest of your great clients who are probably freaking awesome and love what you have done for them.

Sometimes, when there is someone willing to pay us good money, we overlook what our gut is telling us, and we let them in. We forget that, at some point, we will suffer the repercussions.

**Now, "toxic" maybe a little harsh. They may not be bad people, and it is YOUR responsibility to not let others' bullshit affect you.**

BUT, there are only two things that you need to do to avoid letting in clients that are less than ideal.

The first one is SIMPLE....

# TRUST YOUR GUT!

When you are doing a call with a potential new client, keep your eye out for red flags.

■ **LadyBalls**

They may complain: *"I've had seven coaches in the past and none of them did me any good."*

Uber-detailed questions: *"If I go ahead with you, will you be able to help me choose the perfect blue for my sales page button and have it be exactly 950 pixels wide?"*

Relinquishing responsibility: *"If I come on with you, do you GUARANTEE that YOU are going to make ME money?"*

Ooh there's a whoooole other JodyJelas.com show on that puppy. Mentors are your guide and strategist... you still gotta do the work.

The second is a simple 3-column list....

Now, I owe this one to Nat who is on my team. She manages my ass.

In clearing a blank canvas to attract more of the awesome clients, we went to the whiteboard.

Column 1: Good Clients. Column 2: Bad Clients. Column 3: Ideal Clients. (For some reason, putting the GREAT clients on the far right away from the others made it feel better in my head)

## Consistency

Now, go over all your clients in the last six months and put them into one category or another.

Remember, a good client doesn't make an IDEAL client. Think of the ones you LOVED working with—they're ideal.

**Just because they can afford you, doesn't make them ideal or even good. Don't sell yourself short.**

Then go to your list of ideal clients and write down all the reasons they were ideal. Were they get-shit-done people? Action takers who listened and did the work? Were they positive to be around?

Funny?

Most of my best clients actually become my really good friends.

Now, take that list of ideal clients and the reasons they are ideal, and put it on your wall. Revisit it on a regular basis. Keep that ideal person in the forefront of your mind constantly, and watch how you only attract more of those.

■ LadyBalls

Go as far as to create a "wall of fame" in your office of your favourite clients. Like a shrine of appreciation.

## Magnetic Blog—Hot Content Every Time

I have a superpower! I was not born with it, and it was not magically put upon my head in a nerd ceremony.....

I am a SELF-TRAINED and a self-proclaimed expert in the art of seeing a blog post in EVERYTHING.

I'm often heard saying.....

"Hey, there's a blog post in that!"

Now, this power has not always been so. I had to form a new habit.

> Even back when I was text blogging, I would carry around with me a little notebook. I'd have little brain dumping sessions to come up with blog ideas. Then, when I was out and about other ideas would come to me.

## Consistency

Before I knew it, a tsunami of ideas would flood into my head every day. I'd record them into my little notebook and then when it came to writing or scripting my blogs, I had a bunch of ideas ready for me.

I now use a phone app called Trello. This allows me to have four columns:

"TO DO", "RECORDING NEXT", "RECORDED" (ready to edit) and "PUBLISHED".

This way, I keep a flow of all the recent and upcoming posts so I make sure I have a good cross section of Personal Development and actual training of some kind. When coming up with content, it doesn't ALWAYS have to be HOW-TO's or seriousness. In fact, people like to connect with people, so it's actually VERY important to KEEP IT REAL and do a few personal posts.

That way, people can really get to know you and as they know and like you more.... they are more likely to buy your shit!

> Keep in mind you'll get some haters too. Which is AWESOME–because that means you're putting yourself out there.

**LadyBalls**

Your first hater... means you're playing with the big boys! That's how you roll! :)

How-to videos, personal stories, software or book reviews, interviews, case studies, tools, there are sooooo many content ideas. Once you get into the habit of coming up with blog posts... you'll have more ideas than you can poke a stick at....

Oh, and another thing.... IF you're just starting out don't feel you have to write a *War and Peace* length post either. Short and sweet and to the point is best.

If you can teach something in two minutes instead of ten... don't fluff it up... smash it out in two.

---

**DOWNLOAD 21 CONTENT IDEAS**
**It's free over at:**
**www.ladyballsthebook.com/bonuses**

---

# 8

# UPLEVEL THAT SHIT

■ LadyBalls

Whatever you're thinking, think bigger.

It's the choices you make every day and in every moment that matter. Life is just a series of small moments.

Now is a moment... *Now* is a moment...

> How you feel, what you attract into your life, the vibrations you are projecting to those around you, all comes down to now—who you choose to be in THIS moment.

Now, you can have all of the sales funnel strategies and personal development training in the world. You can be surrounded by the most inspiring people in the world or the biggest group of assholes you ever knew... but there is one thing that will remain consistent to the day you die.

The person who you need to make #1 is YOU.

We are all born with limitless power and possibilities. We are gifted with more genius than we can ever crack into in our lifetime. As we grow up, we somehow seem to stifle our creativity and our genius, rather than reveal its power.

No matter what happens in your life, you need to make sure of one thing…

Every decision you make must be one that makes you feel proud of yourself.

Not to please others, not to tell the world, but so that you wake up each day and know in your heart that no matter what happens to you, you know that you can stand strong and be proud of who you are.

We all make mistakes. They're just learning curves. Not everything works out the way we want, but as the *Rolling Stones* said:

> You can't always get what you want, you get what you need.

Every 'up' time is a driver for more good. Every 'down' time is a teacher. There is no light without dark.

# LadyBalls

As long as you stand true to who you are and your values, as long as you make all your decisions from a place of love (especially self love), and that you are proud of yourself... then you will come to the end of your life with zero regrets.

Only love and proudness.

Wherever you are at in your journey, the fact that you have read this book means you are constantly searching to learn and improve your life.

So, I am proud of you.
You got this!

REGISTER FOR MORE FREE
BONUSES OVER AT:

**www.ladyballsthebook.com/bonuses**

www.ingramcontent.com/pod-product-compliance
Lightning Source LLC
Chambersburg PA
CBHW051912170526
45168CB00001B/359